Philosophy of Religion

Philosophy of Religion

for AS students

by Helen F Jeys

Series Editor: Roger J Owen

Dedication
For David, William, and the memory of John Wooldridge.

Roger J. Owen, Series Editor
Roger J. Owen was Head of RE in a variety of schools for thirty years, as well as being a Head of Faculty, advisory teacher for primary and secondary RE, Section 23 Inspector and 'O' Level and GCSE Chief Examiner. Author of seventeen educational titles, he is currently an education consultant and WJEC Religious Studies AS and A2 Chair of Examiners.

Acknowledgements
The author and publishers would like to thank the following for permission to reproduce copyright photographs and other illustrations in this book:
Camera Press Ltd, p. 51 (all images), 52 (centre and left), 55; Celtic Picture Library, p. 11, 52 (top left); Ceri Jones, p. 37; Mary Evans Picture Library, p. 4, 6 (both images), 7, 12, 15 (both images), 25 (both images), 26, 31, 57, 60; National Library of Wales, p. 45; Professor Richard Swinburne, p. 18; The Mary Baker Eddy Collection (Courtesy of), p. 65; Rev Dr. John Polkinghorne KBE, FRS, p. 17; Science Museum/Science & Society Picture Library, p. 41.

Published by UWIC Press
UWIC, Cyncoed Road,
Cardiff CF23 6XD
cgrove@uwic.ac.uk
029 2041 6515

ISBN 1-902724-75-5

Design by *the info group*
Picture research by *Glyn Saunders Jones*
Printed by *HSW Print*

Commissioned with the financial assistance of Awdurdod Cymwysterau, Cwricwlwm ac Asesu Cymru / the Qualifications, Curriculum and Assessment Authority for Wales (ACCAC).

Philosophy
of Religion
for AS students
by Helen F Jeys
Series Editor: Roger J Owen

Contents

Philosophy of Religion

Introduction

This student textbook follows the WJEC/CBAC specification for AS level Religious Studies Module (2b) in Philosophy of Religion. It is designed to be used in conjunction with the teachers' book, which provides suggestions on how to deliver the topics covered and also ways in which students might answer tasks set within the student guide.

This book assumes no prior knowledge of Philosophy of Religion. Nevertheless, it should not be the only book referred to during the course, as Advanced level study requires the skills of wide reading and the analysis of a range of scholarly views on different issues.

Various tasks are set within each chapter and students are encouraged to think about, and discuss, issues pertinent to the topic under consideration. The variety of tasks set reflects the skills developed during Advanced level study. AS level candidates are expected to demonstrate not only knowledge and understanding of key ideas, but also certain skills, such as the ability to sustain a critical line of argument, to justify a point of view, and to relate elements of their course of study to a broader context, as well as to specified aspects of human experience. A glossary of technical terms is given at the end of each chapter to facilitate this knowledge and understanding.

This book, and the accompanying teachers' book, is constructed with Key Skills in mind. Students are asked to develop communication skills by taking part in discussions, gathering information and writing. They are asked to develop ICT skills through encouragement to make critically aware use of the Internet, and to present findings in the form of class presentations. They are asked to solve problems through making cases for particular viewpoints, and to work with others on joint research projects. They are also asked to reflect on their own learning and performance by using the self-assessment sheets provided in the teachers' book.

Many of the arguments presented in this book refer to primary material as a starting point. This aims to enable students to read the arguments in their basic form. The language is undoubtedly difficult, but students' ability to understand philosophical language will improve over time and it is worth persevering in this respect. Students should try to decipher the philosopher's point first-hand, rather than concentrating on secondary material: this helps to bring the subject alive.

The book also attempts to reflect the diverse views that can be held on each argument presented. No view is correct or incorrect, but students are encouraged to support and illustrate their views accurately. Indeed, they should be able to demonstrate awareness that scholarly attitudes are diverse. Various worksheets in the teachers' book will enable students to record the views and quotations of philosophers and this should help in gaining an accurate portfolio of attitudes and views.

Note about language

When studying Philosophy of Religion, you will encounter a number of difficult, confusing terms. Most of them are explained in the text and the glossaries should help to clarify others, but it is important that these technical terms are used in answers.

Note about dates

This book uses the abbreviations CE and BCE for Common Era and Before the Common Era. Some books use AD (Anno Domini) for CE and BC (Before Christ) for BCE. The actual years are the same, only the tag is different.

The Existence of God

Aim of the section

This section will investigate the question of God's existence. Can we prove that God exists? You will be introduced to two major philosophical arguments:

1. The Teleological / Design Argument

2. The Cosmological / Causal Argument

You will also be expected to consider the challenges that could be levelled at each of these arguments and in so doing evaluate their relative success. Are you convinced, after reading each argument, that God exists?

Can We Prove That God Exists?

Aim

This chapter will outline the various problems that arise when the question of God's existence is raised. You will be introduced to the nature of argument and the idea of proof. By the end of this chapter, you should be able to assess whether it is possible to prove the existence of God through the use of logical arguments. This chapter will also introduce you to sociological, psychological and scientific arguments which undermine belief in God.

A survey of the British population was carried out in 1998 by the National Centre for Social Research. The statistics revealed some interesting facts. Over one in five people agreed with the statement "I know God really exists and I have no doubts about it" while only one in ten people said they did not believe in God. During this first section, you will study the reasons why over 20% of the British population have no doubt in their mind that God exists.

Task

Writing task	Define the following terms:
	• Theist
	• Atheist
	• Agnostic

However, before we look at what philosophers such as Thomas Aquinas and William Paley said concerning God's existence, we must first consider the seemingly simple question, can we **prove** that God exists?

The nature of Arguments

Many philosophers believe that we can actually prove that God exists by our abilities to reason and argue. This idea is called **natural theology**. Such philosophers have used arguments in an attempt to prove their ideas.

What is an argument?

When we consider what we mean by the word argument, most of us would think of two or more people rowing over an issue. However, this is not strictly true! According to the Collins English Dictionary, the word also refers to 'a point or series of reasons presented to support or oppose a proposition.' For example:

- The Pope is the Head of the Roman Catholic Church
- John Paul I was a Pope
- Therefore John Paul I was the Head of the Roman Catholic Church

The above three statements make up an argument. The first two statements are called *premises* and the third statement is called the *conclusion*. The reasoning we have used to draw the conclusion from this list of premises is called deductive reasoning. As the first two premises lead logically to the conclusion, we can call this argument valid. Furthermore, each premise is true; we cannot deny the validity of any of the premises. So, this argument is called a proof. In other words, if you were to say that the conclusion was wrong, you would be making no sense!

Look at the following example:

- The Houses of Parliament are in London
- London is in Great Britain
- Therefore the Houses of Parliament are in Great Britain

Again, each of the premises are true and we use our deductive logic to arrive at the conclusion. Therefore, this argument can also be said to be a proof.

Task

Writing task	Make up five proofs of your own. Make sure that each proof fulfils the following criteria:
	1. Each premise must be true
	2. The conclusion must follow on logically from the premises.

Inductive arguments

Read the following argument:

- The sun rises every day
- The sun rose today
- Therefore, the sun will rise tomorrow.

Do you think that the above argument is a proof?

It follows a logical pattern and is quite persuasive. However, it is different from the proofs we have considered before. The conclusion in the above argument is not the only possible one. If you consider the two criteria in the writing task above, this argument does not fulfil the second criteria — the conclusion does not necessarily follow on from the premises. Although it is probable that the sun will rise tomorrow, there is a slight possibility that it will not. The sun could blow up or something could collide with the earth, throwing it off its present orbit of the sun. This argument, therefore, does not use *deductive* reasoning; it uses what we call *inductive* reasoning. In other words, the conclusions such arguments arrive at might be considered *probable* or just *possible*, depending upon one's perspective: we might not all agree as to *how* persuasive an inductive argument is.

Task

Writing task	Make up five inductive arguments of your own.

Seminar topic

Discuss with the rest of your group how persuasive the conclusions of your arguments are.

Arguments for the existence of God

As we have already noted, many philosophers believe in natural theology. In other words, they think that we can use arguments to prove that God exists. For example, consider the following argument that could be used to prove God's existence:

1   A miracle is an event that breaks the laws of nature
2   The only being capable of performing a miracle is God
3   Therefore, God exists.

Is this argument a *proof*? If we consider this argument in the light of what we have learned so far, then it cannot be considered to be a proof. For example, some people may disagree with how the first premise defines the word miracle. Some would define the term as referring to *any amazing coincidence* and would not think that the term has to refer to an event that *breaks the laws of nature*. Furthermore, many people would argue that miracles, quite simply, cannot happen! Such people may argue that there will always be a rational explanation for any occurrence, no matter how strange. As a result, we cannot regard this argument as proof for God's existence.

However, there are other problems associated with trying to prove God's existence. Many people *interpret the evidence differently*. For example, read the following account of a miracle taken from the New Testament:

'When it was evening, the disciples came to him and said, 'This is a lonely place, and the day is now over; send the crowds away to go into the villages and buy food for themselves.' Jesus said, 'They need not go away; you give them something to eat.' They said to him, 'We have only five loaves here and two fish.' And he said, 'Bring them here to me.' Then he ordered the crowds to sit down on the grass; and taking the five loaves and the two fish he looked up to heaven, and blessed, and broke and gave the loaves to the disciples, and the disciples gave them to the crowds. And they all ate and were satisfied. And they took up twelve baskets full of the broken pieces left over. And those who ate were about five thousand men, besides women and children.'

Matthew 14:15-21.[1]

You might have thought that this account of a miracle was sufficient to prove that God's existence is highly probable. However, others amongst you might interpret the account differently. You might have argued that the account is not true. Perhaps the story was made up to convince people of Jesus' power or maybe the story was intended to encourage us to share what we have rather than hoard it for ourselves. Although we are all reading the same account, we are interpreting it in different ways and so arriving at quite different conclusions.

Furthermore, the way in which you interpret the account will depend largely on your starting point. For instance, if you already believe in God before you examine the evidence, you will probably agree with its conclusion. However, if you do not believe in God when you study the account, your conclusion will probably be more sceptical. In other words, the way in which we interpret evidence is not usually objective.

Finally, we do not have any evidence for this miracle other than the accounts we read in the Bible. We cannot talk to eye witnesses or to Jesus himself about the miracle and so it is very difficult to actually prove that the event itself happened. Therefore, to conclude that God exists because of this miracle is impossible.

We can see already that attempting to prove that God exists through the use of logical arguments is extremely difficult and indeed, no philosopher has yet managed to construct an argument which has escaped criticism! Similar to the argument about the sun rising in the morning, any argument concerning the existence of God can only result in a conclusion which is possible or probable. No such argument could be considered a proof.

Seminar topic

How probable do you think the argument for the existence of God based on miracles is?

Does all of your group agree about the success of this argument or do you all disagree?

If there is some disagreement within the group, what do you think this suggests about the attempt to prove God's existence through the use of arguments?

Arguments against the existence of God

It is not only the nature of logical arguments that make proving the existence of God difficult. Some philosophers have argued that God cannot possibly exist. We will consider in the second part of this book the views of those philosophers who believe that the existence of evil and suffering proves that God does not exist. However, at this point, we will consider the views held by such important academics as Karl Marx, Sigmund Freud and Charles Darwin and how their views convince many that God does not exist.

1. Sociological arguments

a. Karl Marx (1818 – 1883)

Karl Marx was the Prussian founder of Communism. He believed that the modern industrial age resulted in the working classes being alienated, oppressed and exploited by the upper classes who became more wealthy at their expense. Marx believed that the only hope the working classes had of attaining social equality was for them to revolt against the upper classes. He was adamant that God did not exist. He said:

Karl Marx

> 'Religion is the sign of the oppressed creature, the heart of a heartless world…it is the opium of the people.'[2]

Marx believed that because religion encouraged people to accept their status in life, this was another way in which the working classes could be oppressed by the rich. Thus, a new society was needed, in which the working classes rebelled against the rich. Marx believed that in such a society, the role of God would be redundant.

b. Emile Durkheim (1858 – 1917)

Emile Durkheim was a sociologist and wrote about religion in his book *The Elementary Forms of Religious Life*, published in 1912. Durkheim thought that belief in God fulfilled a human need; religion was a communal activity and one which was essential for maintaining social cohesion. He states:

> 'When explaining rites, it is a mistake to believe that each gesture has a precise object and a definite reason for its existence. There are some which…merely answer the need felt by worshippers for action, motion, gesticulation. They are to be seen jumping, whirling, dancing, crying and singing, though it may not always be possible to give a meaning to this agitation.'

Although belief in God maintained social unity, Durkheim thought that society had actually invented God in order to confirm society's common beliefs and values. God, rather than having objective and independent existence, reflected the power actually possessed by society itself. Thus, worship of God was, in effect, worship of society. Nevertheless, Durkheim did not believe that the dissolution of religion necessarily meant the same would happen to society. Rather, people within society just had to accept that they should give their respect to society itself, rather than to God. Society was the power that deserved respect, not the God who had been the invention of society.

Task

Research task	Find out what you can about the sociological arguments proposed by Berger and Luckman. Record your findings.

I ♥ MR JOHN lOTS & LOTS

2. Psychological arguments

a. Sigmund Freud (1856 – 1939)

Freud was born in Vienna and is now recognised as the father of psychoanalysis. He believed that the traumas we experience as adults have their foundation in childhood experiences. These experiences are forgotten but remain in the deep recesses of our mind (the id). Freud believed that these experiences could be revealed through dreams and hypnosis.

Sigmund Freud

He believed that the idea of God results from the traumas experienced during our childhood. According to Freud, religious belief helps people to come to terms with the inner conflict caused by such traumas.

Indeed, Freud believed that, just like those people who suffered from obsessive behaviour, believers were equally obsessive in their performance of highly ritual acts, which resulted in feelings of intense guilt if not performed correctly. This led Freud to believe that religion gave people a sense of structure and order within society, as well as hope for future rewards in Heaven.

For Freud, religion enabled people to make sense of the hostile and frightening world around them. The psychological need for God demonstrated by humanity meant that God had no objective existence.

Seminar topic

Do you agree with Freud that religion provides us with a sense of meaning and purpose?

b. Carl Jung (1875 – 1961)

Jung was a Swiss psychoanalyst who worked with Freud for several years. Jung rejected many of Freud's ideas, particularly those concerning the relationship between belief in God and childhood trauma. However, he believed that we are all born with a *personal consciousness* and a *collective consciousness*. The *collective consciousness* refers to the fact that we are all born with a common tendency to create similar mental images. When this consciousness is combined with the knowledge we gain from the world around

Carl Jung

us, we appear to construct similar images. For instance, we all tend to conceive religious images of gods and angels. For Jung, the objective existence of God could not be proven. The only thing he could prove was that God existed as a psychic reality.

In opposition to Freud, Jung believed that this belief in God was able to ensure a mental balance and therefore could even prevent psychological problems from occurring. Nevertheless, Jung could not assert the objective existence of God.

3. Scientific arguments

Since the seventeenth century people have questioned the status of religion in the light of scientific discoveries which have, for many, undermined religious ideas. Many people have the view that science holds a position in direct opposition to that held by religion.

Indeed, the discoveries of some scientists have questioned the very foundations upon which religion has stood for centuries:

a. Nicolas Copernicus (1473 – 1543)

A 16th-century representation of Copernicus' theory.

Before the time of Copernicus, the Biblical view of the world held prominence, even among the scientific community. It was believed that since God had created the universe and placed humans on earth, earth must be at the very centre of the universe. However, Copernicus discovered that, rather than the earth being at the centre of the universe, it was the sun around which the other planets of our solar system revolved. The universe was, then, heliocentric rather than geocentric. In this way, the view held by Christians for centuries was proved to be scientifically inaccurate.

b. Charles Darwin (1809 – 1882)

Evolution from ape to human.

According to the Christian and Jewish story of creation, God made the universe in six days. The sixth day was the climax of creation, for on this day God created humanity. However, this belief was challenged dramatically by the conclusions arrived at by Charles Darwin in his book *On the Origin of Species by Means of Natural Selection*, published in 1859. Darwin concluded that, rather than being created in six days, animals and humanity had evolved over millions of years. Furthermore, evolution was not a designed or planned process, but rather, was the result of completely random and chance variations taking place within nature. Darwin believed that we have all evolved from the primordial soup present after the formation of the earth. Depending on the environment, certain species survived better than others and since the offspring that survived produced more descendants than those who did not survive, over time, this increased the number of offspring with these particular variations. This then assisted the survival of that particular species. Darwin concluded that humanity had evolved through this means of natural selection from apes.

For many philosophers, the idea of God has been used in the past to explain what we were unable to understand about the world around us. This was known as the *God of the Gaps* theory. However, now that many of the gaps in our knowledge of the universe have been filled, we no longer need God. Indeed, in the *Dialogue* article *Religion and Science*, Peter Atkins argued that "God is the terminal illness of reason…God is the last resort of feeble minds masquerading as truth…science…respects the nobility of the human spirit and the ability of collective human brains to achieve true comprehension."[3]

Seminar topic

Do you agree with Atkins' view that "God is the terminal illness of reason"?

Conclusion

We can see that the attempts made by philosophers to prove the existence of God are going to be beset with difficulties. Nevertheless, by the end of this book, you should have a better idea as to where you personally stand. Are the arguments for the existence of God, seen collectively, cumulative proof for the existence of God? Do they prove to you that the existence of God is more probable than not? Or, is the evidence against God through the arguments we have considered above and those considered in Part 2 of the book, too convincing in their attempt to prove that God does not exist?

Task

Writing task	'Attempting to prove the existence of God is a waste of time.' Assess this view.

Glossary

Deductive Reasoning	A form of reasoning used to draw a valid conclusion from a set of logical premises.
Evolution	A theory proposed by Charles Darwin which asserts that animals and humans have evolved from other creatures due to the process of natural selection. The process takes millions of years.
Heliocentric	The scientific view that the sun is at the centre of the solar system. This is in opposition to the view that the universe is geocentric; the theory that the earth is at the centre of the solar system.
Inductive Reasoning	A form of reasoning used to draw one possible conclusion from a set of premises. This form of reasoning is usually based on what we know from experience and more than one conclusion can be drawn from the premises stated.
Natural Theology	A theory stating that we can use our reason to prove that God exists. This is opposed to Revealed Theology which asserts that God's existence is proved through what is given to us by God (e.g. the Bible).
The Id	The term given by Freud to describe the inner most part of the consciousness where memories of childhood traumas are held.

The Teleological Argument

Aim

This chapter will tell you everything you need to know about the Teleological Argument. You will understand what is meant by the word Teleological as well as how the Teleological Argument attempts to prove God's existence. You should be able to understand the argument in various forms, including those proposed by William Paley, David Hume and Thomas Aquinas, as well as how the argument has been updated in more recent times by the likes of Richard Swinburne and John Polkinghorne.

Spot the moth! Camouflage protects it on a silver birch tree.

The complexity and beauty of the universe has never failed to amaze both philosophers and scientists. Just think about the animal world and the ways in which camouflage can save animals from being hunted down by their predators. The stick insect is difficult to spot among dead twigs and plant growth, the tiger easily blends in to the jungle with its stripes, the plaice has the same colouring as the gravel of the river bed and the chameleon can change its colour to fit any background. Many philosophers have wondered just how nature can work in this way; is the complexity and intricacy of nature purely a result of chance or is there something that has designed it this way? This brings us to the Teleological Argument.

The word *Teleological* comes from the Greek word *Telos*, meaning *end* or *purpose*, and therefore seeks to prove God's existence from the end result of the creative process. It is an *a posteriori* argument and therefore uses evidence from the world around us to prove God's existence.

The Teleological Argument is most famously connected with the eighteenth century philosopher and theologian, William Paley.

William Paley (1743-1805)

William Paley was born in July 1743 in Peterborough, England. He graduated from Christ's College, Cambridge in 1763 after training for the Anglican priesthood. He was an orthodox thinker and indeed many of his works became standard text books on the reading list at Cambridge University. His most influential work was published in 1802 and was called *Natural Theology* or *Evidences of the Existence* and *Attributes of the Deity, Collected from the Appearances of Nature*. Paley believed that one could understand something about the nature of God by looking to God's creation of the natural world. William Paley died in 1805.

William Paley

It is in Paley's most influential work that we can read his version of the Teleological Argument. Read the following account and see if you can understand what Paley is trying to say:

'In crossing a heath, suppose I pitched my foot against a stone, and were asked how the stone came to be there, I might possibly answer, that, for anything I knew to the contrary, it had lain there forever: nor would it perhaps be very easy to show the absurdity of this answer. But suppose I had found a watch upon the ground, and it should be inquired how that watch happened to be in that place: I should hardly think of the answer which I had before given, that, for anything I knew, the watch might have always been there. Yet why should not this answer serve for the watch as well as for the stone? Why is it not admissible in the second case, as the watch is in the first? For this reason, and for no other, viz. that, when we come to inspect the watch, we perceive (what we could not discover in the stone) that its several parts are framed and put together for a purpose. e.g., that they are so formed and adjusted as to produce motion, and that motion so regulated as to point out the hour of the day; that if the different parts had been differently shaped from what they are, of a different size from what they are, or placed after any other manner, or in any other order, than that in which they are placed, either no motion at all would have been carried on in the machine, or none which would have answered the use that is now served by it…This mechanism being observed…the inference, we think, is inevitable; that the watch must have had a maker; that there must have existed, at sometime, and at some place or other, an artificer or artificers, who formed it for the purpose which we find it actually to answer; who comprehended its construction, and designed its use.'[4]

So, William Paley argues that if we were to discover a stone upon a heath, it would not be strange to conclude that this stone could possibly have been there forever. However, if we were to come across a watch, we would not come to the same conclusion. Why? Paley concludes that there are two main reasons why we would not conclude that the watch had been there forever:

(1)   The watch has a purpose. The reason why the cogs within the watch work in a very specific way is because the watch has the purpose of telling the time. If the cogs did not work in this way, then its purpose would be very different.

(2)   The watch works in a very specific way; it follows an orderly pattern. Indeed, if the watch worked in a different way, or its internal cogs were arranged in a very different order, then the watch would not serve the purpose of telling the time.

Paley concludes that because this watch has purpose and order, then it must have had a designer; someone who designed the watch with a specific order for the purpose of telling the time. Although the universe is obviously far more complicated than a watch, you can see where Paley is going with his argument. If Paley can conclude that the order and purpose within a watch points to a designer, then the same can be said of the universe. Since the universe reflects a more complicated system of order and purpose, then the only conclusion to come to is that the universe, too, is a result of the work of a designer; this designer being God. You can imagine God as an architect working at His drawing board, designing the universe and all of its intricate parts so that it will work in a perfect orderly way.

Let us think about these two parts of Paley's argument in a little more depth.

Order

What do we actually mean by order? The word implies regularity and things working in a methodical and constant way. Philosophers who agree with the argument would argue that such order could not possibly be a result of chance but rather of the conscious work of a designer being.

There are many examples of order within the universe.   So much of our lives, for instance, revolves around the workings of the seasons.   Just think of how the seasons come and go and how our food cycle depends upon the regularity of the seasons. What would happen if nature did not work in this way? How could we have survived in such a chaotic system? Paley states:

'While the possible laws of variations were infinite, the admissible laws, or the compatible laws compatible with the system, lie within narrow limits. If the attracting forces had varied according to any direct law of the distance, let it have been what it would, great destruction and confusion would have taken place. The direct simple proportion of the distance would, it is true, have produced an ellipse; but the perturbing forces would have acted with so much advantage, as to be continually changing the dimensions of the ellipse, in a manner inconsistent with our terrestrial creation.'[5]

Purpose

Similarly, Paley argues that the universe works as it does for a particular purpose. If we take the example of the working of the seasons for instance, we could conclude that the seasons work as they do so as to produce the correct circumstances to give us crops. Similarly, our bodies work in such an intricate and complicated way to fulfil a purpose; to continue the human race. Paley gives us many examples to illustrate this point. Indeed, the complexity and intricacy of nature appears to fill Paley with a sense of awe and wonder:

> 'The hinges in the wings of an earwig, and the joints of its antennae, are as highly wrought, as if the Creator had nothing else to finish. We see no signs of dimunition of care by multiplicity of objects, or of distraction of thought by variety.'[6]

Paley even states that the eye alone is proof of God's designing power. Just think of the complexity of the human eye and the intricate way in which it is arranged; all of this complexity and intricacy is not there for the sake of it! The way in which the eye works has a very specific purpose: to enable us to see. Similarly Paley discusses the design of human teeth. At birth, every part of the human mouth is perfectly formed but the design is so perfect that nature does not permit teeth to be formed until a time when a baby has usually finished its dependence upon the mother's milk and needs to eat food. This foresight on the part of nature is yet more evidence for Paley that there is a designing mind behind creation.

Paley refers also to the lacteal system to support his view:

> 'The lacteal system is a constant wonder; and it adds to other causes of our admiration, that the number of the teats or paps in each species is found to bear a proportion to the number of the young. In the sow, the bitch, the rabbit, the cat, the rat, which have numerous litters, the paps are numerous, and are disposed along the whole length of the belly: in the cow and the mare, they are few. The most simple account of this, is of thought by variety'.[7]

Seminar topic

Can you think of anything else in the world which appears to have the characteristics of purpose and order?

What would our lives be like if these things did not work in such an orderly manner?

Reading

Read the following quotation by Sir Isaac Newton (1642 – 1727).

> 'Whence is it that the eyes of all sorts of living creatures are transparent to the very bottom…with a crystalline lens in the middle and a pupil before the lens, all of them so finely shaped and fitted for vision that no artist can mend them? Did blind chance know that there was light, and what was its refraction, and fit the eyes of all creatures after the most curious manner to make use of it? These and suchlike considerations always have and ever will prevail with mankind to believe that there is a Being who made all things and has all things in his power, and who is therefore to be feared.'[8]

Seminar topic

Why does Isaac Newton believe in a designing force behind creation? Do you agree with Newton's ideas?

Other versions of the Teleological Argument.

Thomas Aquinas (1225 – 1274)

Thomas Aquinas

Thomas Aquinas became a religious scholar at a very early age. At the age of five, he began receiving his education from Benedictine monks and soon became a diligent student. He went on to attend the University of Naples where he studied Logic and the Natural Sciences. In approximately the year 1242, he became a monk and even though his family tried to tempt him away from the monastic order he continued in the religious life, teaching across Europe. He wrote many important works during this time, including *Summa Theologica*, before dying on 7 March 1274. He was made a Saint in 1323.

In his book *Summa Theologica*, Thomas Aquinas proposed five ways to prove the existence of God. Aquinas' fifth way of proving God's existence was by the Teleological Argument. Aquinas stated that the reason why natural bodies fulfil their function is not a matter of chance but rather as a result of design:

'Now whatever lacks knowledge cannot move towards an end, unless it be directed by some being endowed with knowledge and intelligence; as the arrow is directed by the archer. Therefore some intelligent being exists by whom all natural things are directed to their end; and this being we call God.'[9]

Thus, Aquinas concludes that the cause of this purpose and design is God, since something must be responsible for enabling all natural bodies to achieve their end. For example, a pen can only fulfil its purpose of writing if there is someone to enable the pen to fulfil its function. The pen cannot fulfil this purpose on its own! In the same way, God is the cause of the design of the universe.

David Hume (1711 – 1776)

Even though the Teleological Argument is most famously associated with William Paley, David Hume also wrote about this argument in his book *Dialogues Concerning Natural Religion* which was published in 1779. David Hume wrote his book in the form of a dialogue between Demea, Cleanthes and Philo. It appears that Hume speaks through the figure of Philo who criticises the argument, but nevertheless, during the conversation, Hume pens a valuable version of the argument.

David Hume

Read the following quotation and see if you can understand what Hume is proposing:

> 'Look round the world: Contemplate the whole and every part of it. You will find it to be nothing but one great machine, subdivided into an infinite number of lesser machines…All these various machines, and even their most minute parts are adjusted to one another with an accuracy, which ravishes into administration all men, who have ever contemplated them. The curious adapting of means to ends, throughout all nature, resembles exactly, though it much exceeds, the productions of human contrivance; of human design, thought, wisdom, and intelligence. Since therefore the effects resemble each other we are led to infer, by the rules of analogy, that the causes also resemble; and that the Author of nature is somewhat similar to the mind of man; though possessed of much larger faculties, proportional to the grandeur of the work, which he has executed. By this argument a posteriori, we do prove at once the existence of a Deity, and his similarity to human mind and intelligence.'[10]

Hume compares the world to a machine. Just as a machine contains intricate parts which are so arranged to produce a certain function, so does the world. The world is just a huge machine made up of an infinite number of smaller machines. Therefore, since there are obvious similarities between a machine and the universe, then there must be similarities between the designer of the machine and the designer of the universe. Since the machine has a designer, then so has the universe, even though the designing mind of the universe is far superior to that of the man-made machine.

Seminar topic

Can you spot any similarities between Hume's version of the Teleological Argument and that proposed by William Paley?

Nevertheless, Hume levelled some serious criticisms at this argument and these must be carefully considered before we can evaluate whether the Design Argument is successful in its aim of proving the existence of God. We will come back to Hume's arguments later.

Modern Versions of the Teleological Argument

The Teleological Argument has enjoyed something of a revival in the twentieth century. Nevertheless, you should be careful to note that many modern day scientists and philosophers have updated the argument to reflect the level of sophisticated scientific knowledge we now have.

The Anthropic Principle

The word *Anthropic* originates in the Greek word *Anthropos* meaning *man*. This version of the argument says that the universe is incredibly finely tuned so as to produce life as we know it. Indeed, if anything in the chemical make up of the universe was even minimally different, then life could not have been produced. For example, Arthur Brown states that the ozone layer is of an exact depth to prevent humans from being killed by dangerous rays. Therefore, the ozone layer, he concludes is evidence of a designing mind behind the universe. Paul Davies, in his book *The Mind of God*, goes so far as to argue that the accuracy required at the earliest moment of the Big Bang was equivalent to a marksman hitting a one inch target from a distance of twenty billion light years! The sheer probability of this happening is proof to Paul Davies at least that there has to be a deeper level of explanation for the origin of the universe than the laws of physics.

There are many supporters of this version of the Teleological Argument. Let us just consider two of them: John Polkinghorne and Richard Swinburne.

John Polkinghorne (1930 –)

John Polkinghorne began his career as a physicist but later on in his life trained as an Anglican priest. He took part in a recent Channel 4 series called *Testing God : Killing the Creator*. This is just some of what he had to say: see if you can understand Polkinghorne's main ideas:

John Polkinghorne

'…[A]re the laws of nature in themselves sufficiently self-contained, sufficiently easy to accept as brute fact or do they have features in them which point beyond themselves[?] It seems to me that their rational beauty and their finely tuned fruitfulness are features that do suggest there is more to learn than simply saying, that's the way it happens to be. And it seems to me natural to believe that the rational order and beauty is an expression of a divine mind, and the finely tuned fruitfulness is an expression of a divine purpose.'

For Polkinghorne, the universe is not fixed. Rather, God continually interacts with his creation as a conductor 'conducting the improvised performance of the universe'. However, even though God is an active force within creation even now, all the right circumstances for life to form were present even at the very start of the universe. Polkinghorne's treatment of the Teleological Argument is slightly different from that of Paley and Aquinas. For Paley, even the single occurrence of the eye was proof of a cosmic designer. For Polkinghorne however, it is the very existence and nature of the physical universe that is testimony to a cosmic designer. Polkinghorne believes that God is the 'Total Explanation' for the design of the universe and God's creation is a 'continuing act of creation…through the unfolding process of evolutionary history.'[11]

> **Seminar topic**
>
> **What do you think of Polkinghorne's treatment of the Teleological Argument? Is his argument more or less convincing than other versions you have read about?**

Richard Swinburne (1934 –)

Richard Swinburne also argues in favour of the designed universe. He notes that there are two factors about the universe that are important in arriving at this conclusion:

Richard Swinburne

(1) Swinburne states that the order in the universe is a product of what he calls *regularity of co-presence*. This implies that everything works together in an orderly manner; for example a car works because it consists of an orderly arrangement of mechanical parts, and books can be found in a library because they are arranged in an orderly pattern or arrangement. Swinburne argues that Paley's version of the Teleological Argument focuses on this perspective; thus Paley was impressed largely by the elements of nature which reflected regularities of co-presence.

(2) Secondly, Swinburne argues that the order in the universe is also a product of a *regularity of succession*. In other words, the universe follows an orderly pattern which is, surprisingly, simple. Thus, just as the car is formed in a particular arrangement in order to work, so the driver must follow a simple set of instructions to make this arrangement work. It is this factor that impresses Swinburne the most and convinces him of a designer behind the universe; the universe is very orderly and works according to laws that are independent of us as humans.

Read the following passage written by Swinburne. How does Swinburne's illustration of the victim of a mad kidnapper with the explosive card-shuffling machine demonstrate his ideas?

'Suppose that a madman kidnaps a victim and shuts him in a room with a card-shuffling machine. The machine shuffles ten packs of cards simultaneously and then draws a card from each pack and exhibits simultaneously the ten cards. The kidnapper tells the victim that he will shortly set the machine to work and it will exhibit the first draw, but that unless the draw consists of an ace of hearts from each pack, the machine will simultaneously set off an explosion which will kill the victim, in consequence of which he will not see which of the cards the machine drew. The machine is then set to work, and to the amazement and relief of the victim the machine exhibits an ace of hearts from each pack. The victim thinks that this extraordinary fact needs an explanation in terms of the machine having been rigged in some way. But the kidnapper, who now reappears, casts doubt on this suggestion. 'It is hardly surprising,' he says, 'that the machine draws only aces of hearts. You could not possibly see anything else. For you would not be here to see anything at all, if any other cards have been drawn.' But of course the victim is right and the kidnapper wrong. There is indeed something extraordinary in need of explanation in ten aces of hearts being drawn. The fact that this peculiar order is a necessary condition of the draw being perceived at all makes what is perceived no less extraordinary and in need of explanation. . The teleologist's starting point is not that we perceive order rather than disorder, but that order rather than disorder is there. Maybe only if order is there can we know it is there, but that makes what is there no less extraordinary and in need of explanation.'[12]

Richard Swinburne concludes by arguing from the perspective of probability. He asks the simple question – which explanation for the apparent design of the universe is more likely? Firstly, that the universe reflects all the examples of design due to a random chance event, or secondly that the universe is a product of a conscious designer such as God? Swinburne argues that it is far more probable to argue that the universe is a product of a conscious designer. Swinburne concludes:

'To postulate a trillion trillion other universes, rather than one God in order to explain the orderliness of our universe, seems the height of irrationality.' [13]

Tasks

Research tasks	The following web sites give you more information about William Paley's version of the Teleological Argument. Read through them and make notes on any useful information you find:
	www.philosophers.co.uk/café/rel_one.htm www.philosophyonline.co.uk/pages/teleological.htm
	Also, find out what you can about F R Tennant's Aesthetic Argument and how it relates to the Teleological Argument.

Seminar topic

Do you think that William Paley is successful in proving the existence of God?

Do you think that any of the other versions of the Teleological Argument are more convincing than that written by William Paley?

Glossary

Analogy A technique which uses the similarity between objects to demonstrate a point. In this context, it infers that similarities between man made objects and the universe point to a similar cause; i.e. a designer.

The Teleological Argument – a Success or a Failure?

Aim

This chapter will enable you to understand the major criticisms that have been made of the Teleological Argument. Particular reference will be made to the views expressed by David Hume, Immanuel Kant, John Stuart Mill and Charles Darwin. You should also be able to understand what is meant by terms such as the Epicurean Hypothesis. By the end of this chapter, you should be able to answer an evaluation question on the relative success and failure of the argument.

Many philosophers would argue that the Teleological Argument succeeds in proving the existence of God. After all, it is an argument that uses the evidence of the world around us and thus the argument uses inductive reasoning in order to arrive at its conclusion. Indeed, many of us would agree with the premises that Paley's argument is based upon. For example, most of us would agree that there is order and purpose within nature and that the human race would not exist today had it not been for the precise manner in which the universe was created. We would certainly not be alive if the world did not work according to a system of laws! We could say then that if we agree with Paley's premises, then it is quite reasonable to arrive at his conclusion.

We could also agree with Richard Swinburne's argument from probability. Even if we cannot state categorically that Paley succeeded in proving God's existence through his watchmaker analogy, we could argue that his conclusion is more probable than not. Remember Swinburne's point: if we agree that the conclusion Paley arrives at is more probable than not, then it is rational to agree with his conclusion.

Even those philosophers who oppose the conclusion of the Teleological Argument have praised it for its logic and its ability to bounce back from criticisms that can be made of it. For example, Colin Crowder stated in his *Dialogue* article, *The Design Argument,* that the argument is successful in part because it 'presents itself as vivid, accessible, and 'common-sensical', with its feet firmly on the ground.'[14]

Seminar topic

What do you think Colin Crowder means by this statement? Do you agree with him?

Similarly, Immanuel Kant, a fervent critic of arguments for the existence of God, stated that 'this proof always deserves to be mentioned with respect. It is the oldest, the clearest, and the most accordant with the common reason of mankind.'[15]

Nevertheless, many would argue that the Teleological Argument is not successful in proving the existence of God. Remember, after all, this is an argument attempting to prove that God exists, and as we concluded at the end of the first chapter, many would argue that no logical argument can succeed in doing that.

Seminar topic

What criticisms can you make of the Teleological Argument?

Criticisms of the Teleological Argument

Many philosophers have criticised the Teleological Argument over the years. We will consider the major criticisms made of the argument by David Hume, Immanuel Kant and John Stuart Mill as well as how certain theories such as evolution and the Epicurean Hypothesis succeed in undermining the conclusion arrived at by William Paley.

Seminar topic

Remind yourself of Hume's version of the Teleological Argument!

David Hume (1711-1776)

David Hume, in his book *Dialogues Concerning Natural Religion*, made some devastating criticisms of the Teleological Argument. Indeed, Colin Crowder, in his article *The Design Argument Part 2: Why It Fails* calls Hume's criticisms of the argument 'impressive and daunting.'[16] These criticisms are delivered through the voice of Philo, the character whose views are considered to be the most similar to those of Hume himself. The following points summarise the major criticisms Hume made of the Teleological Argument:

(1) Hume agrees that the fact that there is order in the universe is undeniable. One cannot argue, for instance, that birds have to have wings to fly! However, just because there is order within the universe does not necessarily mean that this order is the result of a creative designing force. The design of the universe could be a result of some completely different cause; we need not necessarily come to the conclusion that God is responsible. After all, the universe could have been the result of a random accident!

Seminar topic

Look back at Swinburne's version of the Teleological Argument and his analogy of the kidnapper and the card shuffling machine. In the light of Swinburne's analogy, how do you think Swinburne would respond to the criticism made by Hume?

The idea that the order we perceive around us is the result of a chance collision of particles of matter is known as the Epicurean Hypothesis. This theory was suggested by the Greek philosopher Epicurus of Samos (341-270 BCE). Epicurus denied the need for any external god to create the universe and believed instead that everything within the universe is a result of pure chance.

According to Hume, therefore, there are several possible causes of the apparent design within the universe and this order need not necessarily be the consequence of a designing mind.

(2) Hume also comments on the analogy used by Paley. Hume considered that the attempt to compare a watch and a watchmaker with the universe and the designer of the universe was rather weak. Can we really compare a watch with a universe and a watchmaker with God? They are slightly different!

Similar effect, similar causes?

Remember, the conclusion of Paley's argument relies upon the success of the watchmaker analogy. If it is a poor analogy, can we really agree with Paley's conclusion? According to Hume, the universe is unique and therefore cannot be compared with anything. Hume says the following through the voice of Philo to Cleanthes:

'If we see a house, Cleanthes, we conclude, with the greatest certainty, that it had an architect or builder; because this is precisely that species of effect, which we have experienced to proceed from that species of cause. But surely you will not affirm, that the universe bears such a resemblance to a house, that we can with the same certainty infer a similar cause, or that the analogy is here entire and perfect. The dissimilitude is so striking, that the utmost you can here pretend to is a guess, a conjecture, a presumption concerning a similar cause; and how that pretension will be received in the world, I leave you to consider.'[17]

(3)   Furthermore Hume argues that Paley's argument is actually illogical. We can agree with Paley that parts of the universe appear to have the characteristics of design and that that would, in turn, point to a designer. However, it would be logically incoherent to conclude that the same is true of the whole universe. Paley, according to Hume, commits the so-called Fallacy of Composition. I would be committing the same fallacy if I suggested that because I have seen one Mexican man wearing a sombrero that I can therefore conclude that all Mexican men wear sombreros! This, obviously, is not true (I think!) The same can be said of the universe. Just because parts of the universe demonstrate qualities of design does not mean that the universe as a whole is also designed. Thus, what is true of a part need not be true of the whole.

Task

Writing task	Make up five statements of your own which commit the Fallacy of Composition.

(4)   Hume questions Paley's conclusion even further. Hume doubts whether Paley's argument actually proves the existence of the god known to Christians, Jews, Muslims or Hindus. Read the following part of the conversation given by Philo and determine what kind of god could be responsible for the design of the universe:

'And what shadow of an argument', continued Philo, 'can you produce, from your hypothesis, to prove the unity of the Deity? A great number of men join in building a house or ship, in rearing a city, in framing a commonwealth: Why may not several Deities combine in contriving and framing a world? This is only so much greater similarity to human affairs.'[18]

Furthermore, if there is a similarity between the designer of the universe and the designer of a watch, then we could also conclude that this god could be mortal and that he could share other similar physical characteristics. God, the designer of our universe, could have eyes, ears and a nose!

Hume goes on to propose that if a god is responsible for the design of the universe, then there is a possibility then that an even more complex being is responsible for the design of that god! Then, an even more sophisticated being could have designed the creator of the god talked about in the conclusion of the Teleological Argument. Where would we end?

Hume also considers the actual design of the universe. Has the universe been designed well at all? For instance, surely if the universe was well designed, we wouldn't have people dying with incurable diseases. And a world of perfect design would not need to have volcanoes and earthquakes, which often cause the deaths of thousands of people. As a consequence, Hume argues, this god is not a good designer at all. If anything, we could agree with Colin Crowder in the second part of his article on the Design Argument who states that 'the Design Argument … points us to a shadowy cosmic architect, not a creator.'[19]

Read the following quotation. What kind of god does Hume think might be responsible for the creation of the world if we agree that the universe is less than perfect?

'This world is very faulty and imperfect, and was only the first rude essay of some infant deity who afterwards abandoned it, ashamed of his lame performance; it is the work only of some inferior deity and is the object of derision to his superiors; it is the production of old age in some superannuated deity, and ever since his death has run on from the first impulse and active force which he gave it…'[20]

Seminar topic

Can you think of any other apparent faults in nature that could make us doubt that the universe is the result of a good design?

(5)   Finally, Hume questions our ability to agree with Paley's conclusion when we were not actually present at the beginning of time to witness what actually occurred. As we were not present at the beginning of creation, then surely, Hume argues we do not have the experience to comment.

Seminar topic

Do you think that David Hume is successful in completely undermining the Teleological Argument? Can any of Hume's points be criticised?

Immanuel Kant (1724 – 1804)

Immanuel Kant had a great deal of respect for the Teleological Argument. However, he did not accept the argument's conclusion. Kant argued that we as humans perceive the universe as being ordered and therefore designed. However, what we consider to be order and design could, in actual fact, be disorder and chaos! We as humans are limited by our human minds and we could be mistaken about our surroundings. Therefore, although Paley's argument is attractive, it is based upon premises that could be entirely inaccurate and, obviously, if the premises upon which the argument is based are found to be false, then we cannot agree with its conclusion.

Immanuel Kant

John Stuart Mill (1806 – 1873)

John Stuart Mill was primarily known for what he said about political philosophy. However, he did comment upon the Teleological Argument and his thoughts are very similar to those we talked about earlier in connection with David Hume. Mill stated that religious people believed that God was all-powerful and all-loving. However Mill believed that these characteristics could not be reconciled with the suffering caused by the forces of nature.

John Stuart Mill

BOY CRUSHED BY FALLING TREE

STORMS HIT BRITAIN

YOUNG HERO
But couldn't save his brother

Suffering caused by the forces of nature.

Mill believed that if God was the kind of god religious people thought he was, then he would not allow his creation to suffer. He would be able to do something that would dilute the effects of such natural forces so that no one would be hurt. Mill stated:

'Nature kills at random and inflicts tortures in apparent wantonness…If the maker of the world can do all that he wills, he wills misery, and there is no escaping that conclusion.'[21]

Seminar topic

Do you agree with Mill that 'there is no escaping' the conclusion that God 'wills misery'?

Charles Darwin (1809 – 1882)

Charles Darwin wrote a book of immense importance. This book is called *On the Origin of Species by Means of Natural Selection* and was published in 1859. We explored Darwin's theory of evolution in the first chapter and indeed many philosophers view this theory as the one most devastating to the conclusion arrived at by William Paley. Such philosophers argue that as we have evolved to suit our environment, then the environment in which we live has not been designed; rather it evolved to be this way.

Richard Dawkins is a modern-day scientist who argues that the theory of evolution means that there is no need for an external designer. He wrote a book called *The Blind Watchmaker* and argued that the apparent design of the universe is simply a result of random chance happenings that occurred within the evolutionary process.

Charles Darwin

For example, Stephen J Gould refers to the panda's thumb which is made up of modified wrist bones. He comments that had this thumb been designed well, it would have looked like the thumb humans have. This would have been of far more use for the panda and its ability to collect bamboo than the thumb it has presently. Thus, rather than the world showing evidence of design, Gould would argue that it reflects evolution; the design is too poor for it to have been planned this way.

Read the following quotation taken from Richard Dawkin's book and see if you can understand why Dawkins thinks that the universe is not designed:

'A true watchmaker has foresight: he designs his cogs and springs, and plans their interconnections, with a future purpose in his mind's eye. Natural selection, the blind, unconscious, automatic process which Darwin discovered, and which we now know is the explanation for the existence and apparently purposeful form of all life, has no purpose in mind. It has no mind and no mind's eye. It does not plan for the future. It has no vision, no foresight, no sight at all. If it can be said to play the role of watchmaker in nature, it is the blind watchmaker.'[22]

Task

Research task	Find out what you can about the evolutionary origins of the species called homo sapiens.
	Remind yourself of the Anthropic Principle. How might this principle be used to oppose those who argue that the theory of evolution proves that God does not exist?

There are a few other theories that some believe undermine Paley's conclusions:

The infinite universe

Many modern day scientists and philosophers argue that the present state of the universe is a result of chance and not a designer being at all. Recently, scientists have proposed that if we live in an infinite universe, then there will have been sufficient universes created in order for one to fulfil all of the criteria necessary for life as we know to it to begin.

Think of it this way: if you give a typewriter to a monkey and an infinite amount of time, then eventually the monkey will write the entire works of Shakespeare. In a similar way, if there are an infinite number of Big Bangs, then eventually there would have been a Big Bang which would have resulted in the universe we have today. In other words, there is no need for a designer to have created the universe; with infinite time, this universe would have been created anyway! It was just a matter of time and just a result of luck.

A monkey + a typewriter + an infinite amount of time = Shakespeare!

The Verification Principle

A more recent philosophical development has been in the area of the language we use. Some philosophers, such as A J Ayer, would argue that if we are not able to suggest ways in which the statements we make can be proved true, then the statement itself cannot be considered meaningful. Therefore, as there are no circumstances under which we can prove the conclusion of the Teleological Argument right or wrong, then we can not possibly say that the conclusion it arrives at is meaningful.

Michael Palmer's Criticism of the Anthropic Principle

Some philosophers are now casting a critical eye upon the modern versions of the Teleological Argument. For instance, Michael Palmer in his recent book *The Question of God*, questions the validity of the Anthopic Principle. (Remind yourself of the Anthropic Principle.)

The Anthropic Principle suggests that the world is finely tuned in order for humanity to be created. God as the creative being is crucial to this fine tuning of the universe. However, Michael Palmer thinks differently. Read the following quotation taken from his book and see if you can understand what Palmer is saying about the Anthropic Principle:

'If the existence of Sophie requires the existence of a particular world, and if Sophie exists, then this particular world exists. True again. However, the truism that this world exists does not mean that this is the only form in which this world could exist: all it implies is that this is the only world necessary for Sophie's existence; that indeed a different world would have meant no Sophie at all. Now admittedly Sophie might be awe-struck by the fact that her contingent existence depends on the world being as it is and not otherwise; but whether this world is or is not an improbable world is not a matter that she can decide. For this decision requires some antecedent knowledge of other possible worlds that allows her to say that this world is improbable – comparable, that is, to a knowledge of other possible throws of the dice that makes the continual throw of a six a calculable improbability – and this she cannot possess because, to adopt Hume's first criticism of the design argument, no comparison with other worlds is possible, given that this world is unique and all that is. If Sophie cannot therefore say whether this world, in comparison with other worlds, is improbable or not, she cannot go on to say that its existence is best explained by a divine intelligence.'[23]

Conclusion

You have been presented with the evidence in favour of, and in opposition to the conclusion arrived at by William Paley. You have to conclude now whether you think that the criticisms made of the Teleological Argument succeed in undermining the validity of the argument. So…

Tasks

Writing tasks	Explain the teleological (design) argument for the existence of God. Evaluate whether the strengths of the argument outweigh its weaknesses.

Glossary

Big Bang	Believed to be the way in which our universe began; a huge explosion of matter which created the raw materials needed to form the universe as we know it today.
Fallacy of Composition	An argument commits this fallacy if it concludes that what is true of the part is also true of the whole.
Homo Sapiens	The evolutionary term used to describe the human race.
Verification Principle	A philosophical theory which proposes that statements can only be considered meaningful if there are circumstances under which they can be proved to be true.

The Cosmological Argument

Aim

This chapter will introduce you to a further argument for the existence of God, the Cosmological Argument, an argument based on change, causality and contingency. After this chapter you should have a good knowledge and understanding of Thomas Aquinas' version of the argument as well as how the argument was developed by other philosophers including Gottfried Leibniz and F R Copleston.

The word *Cosmological* comes from the Greek word *Cosmos,* meaning *universe*. The Cosmological Argument is another argument that uses evidence from the world around us in order to prove that God exists. The evidence the argument refers to is the simple fact that there is a universe.

There are many versions of the Cosmological Argument but the philosopher who is regarded as the one most responsible for its development is Saint Thomas Aquinas. (See p.15)

We can read Thomas Aquinas' version of the Cosmological Argument in his book *Summa Theologica,* where he provided five ways to prove God's existence. We have already encountered the fifth way when we looked at the Teleological Argument. However, the first three ways are known collectively as the Cosmological Argument. We shall consider each of Aquinas' first three ways in turn:

1. The Argument from Change

Aquinas was influenced greatly by the thought of Aristotle (384 – 322 BCE). Aristotle was a great philosopher and was the most famous pupil of Plato. In order to understand the first way, we must briefly look at Aristotle's ideas concerning potential and actual change.

Aristotle proposed that all objects had the potential to change and become different in some way. For instance, he uses the example of a piece of marble which has the potential to become a statue. Aquinas uses the example of wood that has the potential to become hot.

Aristotle, the Greek philosopher, tutors Alexander the Great.

Writing task	List five items around you which have the potential to change into something else. State what these items are and what they have the potential to become.

However, in order for this potential to become actualised, Aristotle believed that a third party had to be involved. For example, if you consider Aristotle's example of the piece of marble becoming a statue, there needs to be a sculptor who can make this change occur. And, with Aquinas' example of the wood having the potential to become hot, there needs to be the agency of fire to actualise this change.

Task

Writing task	Look back at your list of five items which have the potential to change into something else. Now state what third party is needed to actualise this change.

A block of marble becomes a statue, with the help of a sculptor as its efficient cause.

Aristotle called the third party responsible for actualising this potential the *efficient cause*. Aristotle stated that this third party must be in a state of actuality itself in order to fulfil its ability to actualise the potential of other things. If it was merely in a state of potential, then it could not make anything else change. After all, an artist has the potential to become a sculptor but this potential sculptor cannot actualise the potential of a piece of marble to become a statue. The efficient cause in this case has to be a sculptor in order to enable this marble to become a statue.

Read the following extract taken from Aquinas' *Summa Theologica* and try to see how Aquinas uses Aristotle's reasoning to prove the existence of God:

'The first and more manifest way is the argument from motion. It is certain, and evident to our senses, that in the world some things are in motion. Now whatever is moved is moved by another, for nothing can be moved except it is in potentiality to that towards which it is moved; whereas a thing moves inasmuch as it is in act. For motion is nothing else than the reduction of something from potentiality to actuality, except by something in a state of actuality...Therefore, whatever is in motion must be put in motion by another.

If that by which it is put in motion be itself put in motion, then this also must needs be put in motion by another, and that by another again. But this cannot go on to infinity, because then there would be no first mover, and, consequently, no other mover; seeing that subsequent movers move only inasmuch as they are put in motion by the first mover; as the staff moves only because it is put in motion by the hand. Therefore it is necessary to arrive at a first mover, put in motion by no other; and this everyone understands to be God.[24]

Aquinas used Aristotle's reasoning to prove that God exists. Aquinas did not believe in an infinite universe; he believed that there had to be a beginning. As there exists a series of things able to cause movement, then for Aquinas, there needs to be a first mover responsible for the start of this process of movement. Without this first mover, there would be no subsequent movers and, therefore, the universe would not exist today.

This first mover, however, must also be seen as an unmoved mover. It cannot be open to change or be caused to change by anything else; it has to be the very start of the chain of movement. For Aquinas, this first mover was God.

2. The Argument from Cause

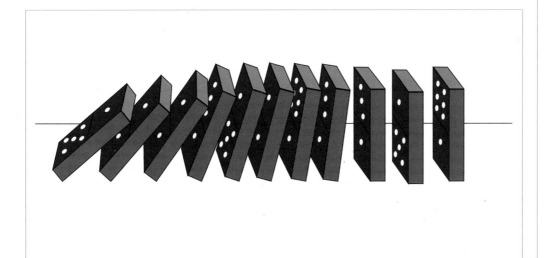

Look at the picture of a series of dominoes falling down, one after the other. Each domino cannot fall down of its own accord: it needs another domino to fall down before it, in order to force it to fall. In this way, one domino causes another domino to fall.

We can see this law of cause and effect everywhere around us. For instance, the cause of the ball moving might well have been the fact that someone kicked it; and the cause of the kick is the movement of the foot on the surface of the ball; and the movement of the foot is caused by the shortening of the tendons in the leg, and so on!

Task

Writing task	State five things in a chain of cause and effect that have resulted in you reading this book today.

Read the following extract taken from Aquinas' *Summa Theologica*. See if you can understand how Aquinas relates the law of cause and effect to the creation of the universe:

'The second way is from the nature of efficient cause. In the world of sensible things we find there is an order of efficient causes. There is no case known (neither is it, indeed, possible) in which a thing is found to be the efficient cause of itself; for so it would be prior to itself, which is impossible. Now in efficient causes it is not possible to go on to infinity, because in all efficient causes following in order, the first is the cause of the intermediate cause, and the intermediate is the cause of the ultimate cause…Therefore it is necessary to admit a first efficient cause, to which everyone gives the name of God.'[25]

Therefore, Aquinas related the law of cause and effect to the universe. Aquinas believed that the chain of cause and effect that exists within the universe could not go back forever; there had to be an ultimate start or cause to the universe – indeed, if everything within nature works according to this law, then why should the universe itself be any different? Furthermore, since things cannot cause themselves, then the cause of the universe must be external to it. Thus, there must be a first cause, and this cause according to Aquinas, was God.

3. The Argument from Contingency

The third way Aquinas proposes in the *Summa Theologica* is known as the argument from contingency. This way is probably the most difficult of Aquinas' ways to understand, but it is believed to be the most persuasive.

It is a fact that everything around us exists contingently; in other words, everything has the possibility of not existing. Think of anything around you at this point – everything you see is contingent; everything will cease to exist at some point in time.

Task

Writing task   List ten things around you that are contingent.

If everything around us is contingent, then there must, conceivably have been a time when none of these things existed. However, as these things exist now and as things cannot cause themselves into existence, then something must have caused things to come in to existence. Aquinas believed that this cause was God. However, God cannot be contingent, for then God would need something else to bring him in to existence. Aquinas stated therefore, that God has necessary existence. In other words God must be incapable of not existing and incapable of being caused by anything or anyone else. Without such a being there would be nothing at all.

Read the following extract taken from the *Summa Theologica* and see if you can follow the argument in Aquinas' own words:

'The third way is taken from possibility and necessity, and runs thus. We find in nature things that are possible to be and not to be, since they are found to be generated, and to be corrupted, and consequently, it is possible for them to be and not to be. But it is impossible for these always to exist, for that which can not-be at the same time is not. Therefore if everything can not-be, then at one time there was nothing in existence. Now if this were true, even now there would be nothing in existence because that which does not exist begins to exist through something already existing. Therefore, if at one time nothing was in existence, it would have been impossible for anything to have begun to exist; and even now nothing would be in existence – which is absurd…therefore we cannot but postulate the existence of some being having of itself its own necessity, and not receiving it from another, but rather causing in others their necessity. This all men speak of as God.'[26]

Each of these three ways concludes in a similar fashion: that God is the uncaused cause and unmoved mover that began the universe. Without this being, nothing could possibly exist. We shall consider in the next chapter whether Aquinas was successful in his attempt to prove God's existence. For now, we shall move on to consider the views of other philosophers who have also contributed to the argument we now call the Cosmological Argument.

The Principle of Sufficient Reason

Gottfried Wilhelm Leibniz (1646 – 1716)

Another important proponent of the Cosmological Argument was Gottfried Wilhelm Leibniz, who based much of his philosophy on the ancient idea of *ex nihilo nihil fit (of nothing, nothing comes)*. Read the following quotation written by Leibniz in his book *Theodicy* (1710) and try to understand the gist of his argument:

> 'Suppose the book of the elements of geometry to have been eternal, one copy always having been written down from an earlier one. It is evident that even though a reason can be given for the present book out of a past one, we should never come to a full reason. What is true of the books is also true of the states of the world. If you suppose the world eternal you will suppose nothing but a succession of states and will not find in any of them a sufficient reason.'[27]

For Leibniz there has to be a reason or cause for everything that exists. Things do not just happen without good reason! Now, if we were to suppose that the universe was infinite and there was no initial starting point, then for Leibniz, this did not provide a sufficiently good reason for the universe's existence. For Leibniz, there had to be an explanation for the universe, a reason or cause and so, just as the book must have a cause for its existence, then so must the universe. This cause was itself uncaused with the reason for its existence being within itself. This uncaused cause of the universe, Leibniz took to be God.

The Kalam Argument

The word *Kalam* comes from the Arabic meaning *argue* or *discuss* and is a version of the Cosmological Argument originating within Muslim circles from about 850 CE. The argument has enjoyed a recent revival through the work of William Lane Craig and Ed Miller. The Kalam Argument proposes that the fact that everything has a cause is a simple law of the universe. As a consequence, we must also conclude that the universe has a cause. Supporters of the Kalam Argument believe that this cause must be distinct from its effect. Therefore, if the cause of the universe is different from the universe itself, then the cause of the universe must be non-physical in nature. This cause is God.

The modern versions of the Kalam Argument rely upon an understanding of the word *infinity*.

We will consider two definitions of the word infinity. If we are to subscribe to the theory that the universe is actually infinite, then we would argue that there is an infinity of time between each second of time. Imagine a library which contains an infinite number of books. Then according to the definition of infinity as actual, if you took out one book, then there would still be an infinite number of books remaining.

You might have guessed, but in terms of time being actually infinite, then you would not actually be able to arrive at the present moment! If an infinite amount of time exists between each moment of time, then one would not be able to reach the next moment of time. Think of it this way:

Let us suppose that a man walks half of the distance from (a) to (b) in one hour. In the next hour, this same man walks half of the remaining distance (i.e. he has now walked three quarters of the entire distance between (a) and (b)). In the next hour, he walks half of the remaining distance and so on and so on. This man would never reach his destination since no matter how many hours he had been walking, there would always be some remaining distance to travel, no matter how small. This is called Zeno's

Seminar topic

What do you think is meant by the word infinity? Can the word infinity be adequately defined?

Seminar topic

'If we are to subscribe to the theory that the universe is actually infinite then we would argue that there is an infinity of time between each second of time.'

Can you spot any problems in thinking that time is actually infinite?

Paradox and demonstrates the notion of infinity being actual. Think of the place (b) being the present time. If time was actually infinite, then the present moment would never be reached, just as the man would never be able to reach his final destination in Zeno's Paradox.

A man and a tortoise illustrate Zeno's Paradox.

Others would agree with the definition of infinity as being potential in nature. In other words, there was a beginning to time and this time continues forward infinitely. Think of how our counting system begins with the number 1 and continues on infinitely (1, 2, 3, 4...) This could be the same with time; there is a start and therefore we would reach this present moment in time. However, we could still anticipate an infinite amount of time in front of us.

> *Seminar topic*
>
> *Which definition of infinity do you think is the most realistic? Why?*

William Lane Craig, in his book, *The Kalam Cosmological Argument* (1979), used these definitions of the word infinity in order to prove the existence of God. His argument can be summarised in the following major points:

1. The present moment exists.
2. Therefore, time cannot be actually infinite.
3. This means that the universe must have had a start.
4. In order to have come into existence, the universe must have been caused to exist.
5. This cause is God.
6. As God chose to create this world then God must be a personal being.

As Craig states:

> 'If the universe began to exist, and if the universe is caused, then the cause of the universe must be a personal being who freely chooses to create the world...the kalam cosmological argument leads to a personal creator of the universe.'[28]

Richard Swinburne

We have come across Swinburne's arguments before when we studied the Teleological Argument. Swinburne also supported the Cosmological Argument in its attempt to prove the existence of God. Swinburne argues that the Cosmological Argument is an effective argument for the existence of God as the explanation this argument provides for the cause of the universe is simpler than any other proposition.

The interesting fact about Swinburne's argument is that he does actually acknowledge the possibility that there might not be a start to the universe. The universe, he admits, could have always been here. Nevertheless, Swinburne argues that God as the cause of matter and time, continues to cause time and matter throughout the passage of time. In other words, the creation of the universe is not a one-off event but is continual throughout time and therefore God continues to create throughout time. The Jewish idea of Shekinah is relevant here. For Jews, God is present at all times and if God were to cease to exist then the universe would also cease to exist. The universe relies upon God's continual creation for its very existence. F R Copleston agrees, stating that God is a *cause in esse*: one which sustains its effect continually. The existence of God therefore is essential for the continued existence of the universe.

F R Copleston

A modern version of the Cosmological Argument was given by F R Copleston on a radio programme broadcast in 1948. It was published in *Humanitas* in the autumn of 1948. He argued that:

1. Everything that exists now has been caused to exist by external causes. (In other words, your file of notes do not cause themselves, they had to be caused by you i.e. an external cause).
2. The universe works in the same way – it must have a cause and this cause must be external to itself.
3. This cause, according to Copleston, is not contingent, but necessary, 'a being that must exist and cannot non-exist.'. Copleston believed that this being had the reason for its existence within itself and was God.

The following quotation given by Copleston demonstrates the idea that there could not a contingent cause of the universe and uses the method of analogy in a most memorable way:

'I don't believe that the infinity of the series of events – I mean a horizontal series, so to speak – if such an infinity could be proved, would be in the slightest degree relevant to the situation. If you add up chocolates to infinity, you presumably get an infinite number of chocolates. So if you add up contingent beings to infinity, you still get contingent beings, not a necessary being. An infinite series of contingent beings will be, to my way of thinking, as unable to cause itself as one contingent being.'[29]

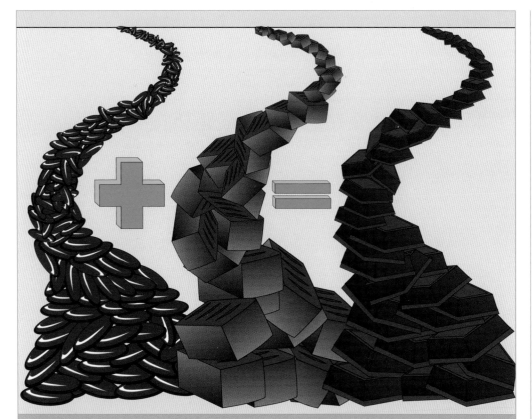

An infinite amount of chocolates + an infinite amount of chocolates = an infinite amount of chocolates.

Conclusion

As we have seen, the Cosmological Argument is a rather general title to describe many different arguments. Each of these versions however, argues that God is a necessary being who was the initial cause of the universe but also continues to cause the matter that exists around us. It is a hugely important argument for the existence of God and even Kant, who was largely sceptical about the validity of such arguments, stated that it is 'the most convincing not only for common sense but even for speculative understanding. It also sketches the first outline of all the proofs in natural theology, an outline which has always been and always will be followed, however, much embellished and disguised by superfluous additions.'[30]

We will consider the accuracy of Kant's conclusion in the next chapter.

Seminar topic

Do you think that Thomas Aquinas is successful in proving the existence of God?

Do you think that any of the other versions of the Cosmological Argument are more convincing than that written by Thomas Aquinas?

Glossary

Cause in esse	A cause which continually sustains its effect.
Contingent	Something which has the possibility of not existing – i.e. finite / mortal.
Necessary	Something which does not have the possibility of not existing.
Shekinah	A Jewish belief in the continual presence of God.

The Cosmological Argument - a Success or a Failure?

Aim

By the end of this chapter, you should have a good knowledge and understanding of all the major criticisms that have been made of the Cosmological Argument. You should be familiar with the criticisms made by philosophers including David Hume, Immanuel Kant and Bertrand Russell and therefore be able to evaluate the relative success of the argument.

Just like the Teleological Argument, the Cosmological Argument uses evidence from the world around us to conclude that God exists. For example, most of us would agree with Aquinas' premise that everything around us has a cause. Therefore, many would argue that because of this fact, the argument must be partly successful in proving the existence of God.

Furthermore, there are modern day scientists who do not undermine the conclusion arrived at by Aquinas.

Seminar topic

Remind yourself what is meant by inductive reasoning.

How would your use of inductive reasoning enable you to agree with the conclusion arrived at by Aquinas?

Reading

Read the following quotation taken from Stephen Hawking's book *A Brief History of Time*. Why does Hawking agree that there could indeed be a being responsible for the creation of the universe?

'With the success of scientific theories in describing events, most people have come to believe that God allows the universe to evolve according to a set of laws and does not intervene in the universe to break those laws. However, the laws do not tell us what the universe should have looked like when it started – it would still be up to God to wind up the clockwork and choose how to start it off. So long as the universe had a beginning, we could suppose it had a creator.'[31]

Stephen Hawking

Nevertheless, there are many philosophers who would argue that there are too many criticisms that can be made of this argument for it to be considered a success. However, before we dive into the criticisms of the Cosmological Argument made by various philosophers, let us begin by considering your views of the argument.

Seminar topic

What criticisms can you make of Aquinas' versions of the Cosmological Argument?

Do you think that these criticisms undermine the success of Aquinas' arguments?

What criticisms can you make of the other versions of the Cosmological Argument?

Are these other versions of the argument less easily undermined than those proposed by Aquinas?

Let us first of all consider some of the criticisms made of each way proposed by Aquinas in his version of the Cosmological Argument.

Before exploring the criticisms that can be made of the argument re-familiarise yourself with each of Aquinas' ways:

The Argument from Change

Aquinas' argument from change is based on Aristotelian logic. However, many scientists would argue that Aristotle's ideas are now completely out of date. For example, many scientists would say that there is nothing that is at a constant state of rest or potential. Rather, it would be more accurate to state that everything is always changing. If this is the case, then the premise upon which Aquinas bases his first way is undermined and thus, we cannot agree with his conclusion.

The Argument from Cause

John Stuart Mill, in his article, *Theism*, agreed with Aquinas' theory that everything around us has a cause. However, to state that the cause of the universe was itself uncaused is a contradiction. To say this more simply, if God is the cause of the universe, then it makes sense to ask, 'what or who caused God?' For Mill therefore, 'our experience, instead of furnishing an argument for a first cause, is repugnant to it.'[32]

The Argument from Contingency

The argument from contingency states that as everything around us is contingent, then there must have been a point in time when everything did not exist. However, we could question whether there was in fact an exact point in time, when everything did not exist. We can admit that there was a time when each individual thing did not exist, but to conclude that there was a point when everything did not exist at exactly the same time, does appear to be slightly inconsistent.

Let us now consider some of the more general criticisms that have been made of Aquinas' three ways:

David Hume

As with the Teleological Argument, the most well known critic of Aquinas' Cosmological Argument is David Hume. Hume's criticisms were first set out in his *Dialogues Concerning Natural Religion* which was first published after his death in 1779. The major criticisms Hume makes of the argument can be summarised as follows:

(1) Hume states that Aquinas' version of the Cosmological Argument commits the Fallacy of Composition: look back at chapter 3 on the success and failure of the Teleological Argument and remind yourself of what is meant by the Fallacy of Composition.

For Hume, just because everything around us has a cause does not mean that the same can be said for the universe as a whole. We shall look at the points made by Bertrand Russell later, but it is worth noting that he agreed with Hume on this point. Russell stated:

'Every man who exists has a mother, and it seems to me your argument is that therefore the human race has a mother, but obviously the human race hasn't a mother – that's a different logical sphere.'[33]

(2) Hume also argues that Aquinas might well have been mistaken in thinking that there had to be a start to the universe. Indeed, our understanding of the laws around us is a result of experience, and therefore we have come to expect that everything around us has a cause. We believe that the sun will rise tomorrow because we have seen it happen every day and we expect that the same will happen tomorrow. However, Hume reminds us that we might be wrong; can we prove conclusively that the sun will rise tomorrow? Indeed, we cannot – and, as a consequence, we cannot know that our experience of the world around us today can be applied to the beginning of the universe. We do not have any experience of the creation of any other universes to conclude that our universe does indeed have a cause.

As a consequence, Hume considers the possibility that the universe could be infinite and therefore, for the process of cause and effect, to have always been in existence. Thus, there could, according to Hume, be an infinite regress of cause. If this is the case, then there would be no start to the universe and therefore, there would be no need for an external cause of the universe, i.e. God.

Anthony Flew agrees with Hume's point here. In fact, he states that Aquinas' idea that there had to be a start to the universe is 'a peculiarly gross howler.'[34]

Furthermore, if there was a start to the universe, then why couldn't the universe have caused itself? Again, Hume questions the need for an external cause for the universe. If God is supposed be self-caused and began the universe, why can we not simply give the same characteristics to the universe itself? Hume states:

'But farther; why may not the material universe be the necessarily existent Being, according to this pretended explication of necessity?'[35]

(3) Hume also argues with Aquinas' conclusion that God is supposed to have necessary existence. For Hume, this is inconsistent since everything that is said to exist, does so contingently. Therefore, to say that God is in some way different is illogical. Indeed, it is contradictory to say that there is something that exists that does not possess the possibility of not existing! Indeed, why should the cause of the universe not be contingent like the causes of everything around us today?

Seminar topic

Many would argue that the criticisms made by Hume of the Cosmological Argument completely undermine its foundations. Do you agree with this view?

Immanuel Kant

The view held by Immanuel Kant towards the Cosmological Argument is very similar to the one he held towards the Teleological Argument. In his *Critique of Pure Reason* (1781) Kant argues that we can only know things about the world around us for we experience these things every day. However, we have no direct experience of the creation of the world and, therefore, we cannot even consider the possibility of knowing anything about it. For Kant, therefore, to try to arrive at a conclusion about the beginning of the universe 'has no meaning whatsoever.'[36]

Furthermore, the argument from contingency concludes that God is a necessary being. However, philosophers such as Kant would disagree that the idea of necessity can be applied to a being that exists. Kant argued that the word necessary can be applied to statements that could be considered tautological, or as self-defining, such as 2+2=4, but not to beings. To state that a being is necessary contradicts all reason and experience.

Seminar topic

Do you agree with Kant that to state that a being is necessary contradicts all reason and experience?

Task

Research task	Some philosophers argue that Kant is incorrect in his criticism of Aquinas' use of the word 'necessary'. They argue that Kant has misunderstood Aquinas' use of the word.
	Find out what you can about the definition of the word 'necessary'.
	From your research, do you think that Kant was correct to criticise Aquinas in this way? (Completing research on Swinburne's support of the Cosmological Argument will help you to answer this question).

F R Copleston and Bertrand Russell's Debate

As stated in the previous chapter, Copleston gave his support for the Cosmological Argument during a radio programme, broadcast in 1948. The broadcast was in the form of a debate between Copleston and another important twentieth century atheist philosopher, Bertrand Russell (1872-1970).

Bertrand Russell meets local people on a visit to Minfordd, Wales.

Bertrand Russell argued that Copleston was incorrect to support the Cosmological Argument. Russell made several important points:

(1) Firstly, he agreed with Kant that it was illogical to use the word necessary when connected with a being. He stated:

> 'The word "necessary" I should maintain, can only be applied significantly to propositions…the difficulty of this argument is that I don't admit the idea of a necessary being and I don't admit that there is any particular meaning in calling other beings "contingent". These phrases don't for me have a significance except within a logic that I reject.'[37]

(2) Secondly, similarly to Hume, Russell argued that the whole idea of cause is derived from our experience of things around us. However, we cannot use this experience to conclude that the whole universe has a cause. This again, according to Russell, is illogical.

(3) In fact, Russell could not agree with Copleston that the universe had to have a cause or an explanation at all! Indeed, Russell stated that the universe might be nothing more than a brute fact. He stated:

> 'I should say that the universe is just there and that's all.'[38]

Seminar topic

What do you think Russell means when he describes the universe as a brute fact?

Do you agree with Russell's view? Why?

In this way, Russell rejected Leibniz' principle of sufficient reason. For Russell, and for other philosophers such as J. L. Mackie, it is questionable whether indeed the universe had to have some ultimate reason for its existence. For such philosophers, it is not illogical to conclude that the universe is absolutely pointless.

(4)   Russell also argued in support of the idea of an infinite regress of cause, refusing to accept the theory that there had to be a first cause to the universe:

Modern Scientific Theories

Before we finish this chapter, we must look at two important scientific theories which many consider succeed in undermining the Cosmological Argument.

Indeed, we have to remember that from a scientific point of view, Aquinas lived in an unsophisticated world. Aquinas did not have the benefit of modern day technology and therefore, it is reasonable that Aquinas' conclusions could well be undermined by modern day science.

1.   The Big Bang

We have already looked briefly at the theory of the Big Bang in relation to the Teleological Argument. As it is a scientific theory concerning the origin of the universe, it is also relevant in our evaluation of the Cosmological Argument. Many philosophers and scientists would argue that there was indeed a start to the universe. However, there is no need for God to cause the universe for the cause of the universe was the Big Bang.

Did a Big Bang like this cause the universe?

Task

Research task	Find out any evidence you can which would support the conclusion that the Big Bang was the cause of the universe.

2. Quantum Physics

While discussing his views of the Cosmological Argument with Copleston, Bertrand Russell stated:

'As for things not having a cause, the physicists assure us that inidividual quantum transition in atoms have no cause.'[39]

Indeed, some modern scientific theories would support the conclusion that in fact, not everything needs a cause. Discoveries by quantum physicists would conclude that certain things, such as electrons, can come in and out of existence without any need of a cause. If this is the case, then why does the universe have to be any different? It too could have popped into existence without any need for an external cause.

Conclusion

So, we have considered many points that both support and oppose the conclusion arrived at by Thomas Aquinas. For many philosophers, the argument simply does not succeed in proving the existence of God. Indeed, if the argument did succeed, what kind of God would be the cause of the universe according to Aquinas? This God would be a necessary being but does Aquinas' argument succeed in proving that God is loving and moral, as the major world religions suggest? However, Jonathan Webber, in his *Dialogue* article, *Cosmological Arguments for the Existence of God: An Introduction* states:

'However, it may be argued that the understanding of God as Creator is part of the traditional understanding and does not contradict any of the other traditional divine attributes; if you can see a long grey trunk protruding from the bushes, there is probably an elephant attached.'[40]

As we have seen, one's opinion of the argument depends upon one's original standpoint. If you already believe in God, then this argument will probably support your beliefs and give your ideas some intellectual justification. However, for those who begin with the standpoint of no faith at all, then this argument will probably not convince them that God exists.

For some philosophers, the Cosmological Argument is successful in that it is based upon our own experience of the world. However, as Michael Palmer points out, this same

Seminar topic

Can you think of any ways in which we could agree both with the creation of the universe being as a result of the Big Bang, and with God being the cause of the universe?

Seminar topic

What do you think Jonathan Webber means when he states that 'if you can see a long grey trunk protruding from the bushes, there is probably an elephant attached'?

Seminar topic

Do you think that the Cosmological Argument succeeds in proving God's existence or do you agree with Michael Palmer that the argument 'ends...in the world of pure speculation'?

argument is doomed to failure because Aquinas concludes by discussing an area of our existence we know very little about. He states:

> 'The Cosmological Argument thus begins in the world of sense and ends…in the world of pure speculation…That God exists is, of course an article of faith; but it is also, according to Aquinas, a proposition capable of proof by the natural light of reason. But in this…Aquinas was mistaken. The existence of a necessary being cannot be demonstrated.'[41]

Arguments Proving the Existence of God - Conclusion

Despite the fact that it is highly unlikely that we will ever encounter a proof for the existence of God, some philosophers suggest that because there are so many arguments for God's existence, the conclusion that God does exist is more probable than not. Richard Swinburne, for example, argues that the amount of evidence that can be provided in favour of God's existence must make us conclude that God's existence is highly probable.

Seminar topic

Do you agree with Swinburne that the existence of God is highly probable?

Tasks

Writing tasks	Explain the cosmological argument for the existence of God.
	Assess how far it is possible to prove the existence of God by reasoned argument.
	Outline the cosmological argument for the existence of God and explain why some philosophers have rejected it.
	Discuss how far the cosmological argument is a strong argument for the existence of God.

Glossary

Infinite regress of cause	The process of cause and effect going back infinitely; needing no primary cause.
Tautology	A statement that is self-defining, such as 2+2=4, or the definition of a batchelor as an unmarried man.

Evil and Suffering

Aim of the section

The second section of the book considers the nature of evil and suffering. It will ask you to consider whether the presence of pain proves that God does not exist.

You will be introduced to the views of those who attempt to defend God against such challenges, in particular, those of Augustine and Irenaeus. As in Section 1, you will be expected to evaluate the relative success of such defences.

After studying each of them, do you think that evil and God can co-exist?

The Nature of Evil

Aim

By the end of this chapter, you should understand what is meant by the words evil and suffering and you will recognise the distinction between moral and natural evil.

Every time you pick up a newspaper or watch the news on the television, you will be faced with images of people suffering and of the evil that people have committed. Suffering and the consequences of evil are inescapable; we are surrounded by them and it is difficult to understand how and why they happen and what we can possibly do to rid the world of terrible tragedy. Firstly, we must understand the various types of evil that occur in the world today.

Moral Evil

Look at the following images:

Victims of the Vietnam War; Kosovan refugees; New York on 9/11.

These pictures represent what is known as *moral evil*. These are acts of evil caused by the actions of human beings. The suffering caused by such acts of evil is often difficult to understand because it is the result of actions caused by people like ourselves. Often, such acts appear to have no motive whatsoever and it is difficult to understand why they happen.

We only have to think of the recent case of the late Dr. Harold Shipman to demonstrate the evil that mankind can be responsible for. He managed to avoid being caught for many years, during which he took the lives of hundreds of his patients by issuing them with lethal doses of drugs. He was sentenced to life imprisonment and commited suicide in prison so that it is still not known exactly how many deaths he was responsible for.

A horrific embodiment of moral evil can also be seen in the example of the Holocaust, where approximately six million Jews, homosexuals, gypsies and disabled people were killed under the orders of Adolf Hitler. Such depravity is a lesson to us all about the potential evil mankind is capable of.

Natural Evil

Look at the following images:

Floods in North Wales; the aftermath of an earthquale in Japan; famine in Sudan.

The above pictures represent what is called natural evil. Such evil is caused by events that happen within nature and are not controlled by humans. These events happen when nature is believed to malfunction in some way. Again, incredible suffering can be caused by natural evil: earthquakes can devastate whole cities and the many floods that have taken place over the last few years have caused innumerable deaths and resulted in whole communities being made homeless. For example, in 1755 an earthquake took place in Lisbon on the 1st of November, resulting in the deaths of up to a fifth of the entire Lisbon population. An earthquake that occurred in Tokyo on 1 September 1923 resulted in the deaths of 100,000 people.

Disease is another kind of natural evil. Two of the most devastating diseases, which claim millions of lives across the globe each year, are cancer and AIDS. For example, it is estimated that by the end of the year 2001, approximately 24.8% of all pregnant women in South Africa were infected with the HIV virus.[42] Whether such diseases are always wholly natural evils, however, is a subject of heated debate. Some would argue that sometimes they may be caused by human behaviour - such as smoking cigarettes, creating environmental pollution and promiscuous sexual behaviour. If so, some diseases may be a combination of natural evil and moral evil.

From a religious and philosophical point of view, both of these types of evil cause problems for those who believe that God exists. We shall consider these problems in the next chapter.

Task

Research task	Read through one daily newspaper. Write down every example you can find of instances of moral and natural evils.

Seminar topic

What kind of suffering do you think each type of evil creates?

When you read about examples of evil and suffering, what emotions do you feel?

Does reading about natural evil make you feel any differently from reading about examples of moral evil?

The Problem of Evil

Aim

By the end of this chapter, you should understand why the presence of both moral and natural evil cause philosophical problems for the existence of God. You will understand what is meant by the phrase The Problem of Evil. The chapter also includes a section on the problems encountered with considering the subject of animal suffering.

Read the following passage written by Elie Weisel, a survivor of the Holocaust:

'Never shall I forget that night, the first night in camp, which has turned my life into one long night, seven times cursed and seven times sealed. Never shall I forget that smoke. Never shall I forget the little faces of the children, whose bodies turned into wreaths of smoke beneath a silent blue sky. Never shall I forget those flames which consumed my faith forever. Never shall I forget that nocturnal silence which deprived me, for all eternity, of the desire to live. Never shall I forget those moments which murdered my God and my soul and turned my dreams into dust. Never shall I forget these things, even if I am condemned to live as long as God Himself. Never.'[43]

Seminar topic

What kind of evil is Elie Weisel referring to in the passage above – natural or moral?

Why does Weisel say that his experience during the holocaust murdered [his] God?

In your view, do you think that God was in any way responsible for what happened to Elie Weisel?

For many philosophers over the centuries, the existence of such evil causes real problems. According to the traditional world religions, God is meant to be omnipotent (all powerful), omniscient (all knowing), omnipresent (everywhere) and omnibenevolent (all loving). Some would argue therefore that these characteristics of God are not compatible with the existence of evil and suffering in the world. Seemingly, there is an inconsistency between the evil and suffering within the world and the existence of an all powerful and all loving God.

For example, if God is meant to be all powerful, then He could surely do something to prevent people from committing acts of evil. He could stop them from doing so, or He would be sufficiently powerful to make sure that such people were not created in the first place! If God was powerful enough to create the world, then He could have ensured that the world He created was perfect. As God is also believed to be omnipresent, then God would know what was happening in every part of the world and would therefore know where evil was happening and would be able to do something about it. Finally, as God is meant to be all-loving, He would care about His creation and would want to prevent them from being hurt. Many people believe that He does none of these things.

Seminar topic

Discuss how God's omnipotence, omnipresence and omnibenevolence are incompatible with the existence of natural evil.

Philosophers who agree that such an incompatibility exists would argue that there are two possible conclusions:

1. God does not exist. After all, if God were to exist, He would not tolerate such evil taking place.

2. God should be understood rather differently. God cannot be omnipotent, or omniscient or omnibenevolent. Therefore, we must redefine what me mean by the word God.

Seminar topic

Which conclusion do you agree with?

Do you think that you have to agree with one of the above conclusions or is there a third possibility?

An early Christian writer called Lactantius, quotes Epicurus (341-270BCE), who summarised the so-called Problem of Evil in the following passage. It is quite a tongue twister!

> 'God either wishes to take away evils, and is unable; or He is able, and is unwilling or He is neither willing nor able; or He is both willing and able. If He is willing and is unable, He is feeble, which is not in accordance with the character of God; if He is able and unwilling, He is envious, which is equally at variance with God … if He is both willing and able, which alone is suitable to God, from what source then are evils? And why does He not remove them?'[44]

Task

Writing task	In your own words summarise the main points Epicurus is making in the above passage.

Similarly, David Hume set out the problem in his *Dialogues Concerning Natural Religion*. He concluded that either God was not omnipotent, or omnibenevolent, or that evil did not exist. As Hume could not argue with the existence of evil, and as both omnipotence and omnibenevolence were crucial characteristics of God, then the only conclusion to arrive at was that God did not exist. His solution then, was atheism.

An important literary text that discusses the problem of evil is called *The Brothers Karamazov* written by Fyodor Dostoyevsky in 1880. In this book, one character called Ivan discusses the problems caused by suffering with his brother Alyosha who is a novice priest. The brothers discuss the true story of a six-year-old boy who threw a stone at a dog belonging to a local landowner. In front of his mother, the boy was stripped naked and forced to run before a pack of dogs. The dogs chased him down and savaged him to death. Ivan concludes that the suffering which God does nothing about '[is] too high a price' to pay.[45] Although Ivan does not deny the existence of God, he does not want to play any part in God's plan for humanity.

Seminar topic

Do you agree with Ivan's conclusion?

Many people, however, would not agree with Ivan's conclusion. Rather, many would argue that evil can exist alongside God and that the presence of evil is not necessarily incompatible with His existence. Such philosophers have proposed what we call *Theodicies* (originating from the Greek *Theos*, meaning *God*, and *Dike*, meaning *justification*). In other words, Theodicies justify God's existence alongside the presence of evil. We will consider two of the most important theodicies, those proposed by Augustine and Irenaeus, in the next chapter.

Animal suffering

Before concluding this chapter, it is important to make special note of the unique problems encountered when discussing the suffering experienced by animals.

The major problem with the issue of animal suffering is quite simply that animals are not the same as humans! Although some animal suffering is due to the animal instinct to survive, most philosophers acknowledge that much animal suffering is not the fault of the animals themselves. A lot of suffering experienced by animals is due to humans. Think of the examples of animal abuse we see on television programmes and the pleas made by dogs' homes not to buy dogs at Christmas because of the number of animals abandoned after the holiday season. We cannot forget vivisection also, and the amount of suffering caused by humans on animals in the name of medical progress.

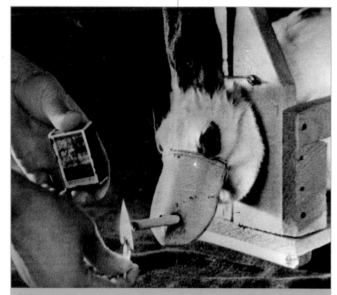

Experiments on animals, carried out for medical research.

Although many would argue that this experimentation is for the greater good of humanity, there is no denying that it causes suffering. Indeed, religious believers think that humans were made to be stewards of God's creation and in this way were meant to take care of the world and its inhabitants.

Peter Singer is a well-known supporter of animal rights. Read the following quotation and try to understand what Singer is arguing:

'In the past, argument about vivisection has often missed the point, because it has been put in absolutist terms. Would the abolitionist be prepared to let thousands die if they could be saved by experimenting on a single animal? The way to reply to this purely hypothetical question is to pose another. Would the experimenter be prepared to perform his experiment on an orphaned human infant, if that were the only way to save many lives? …If the experimenter is not prepared to use an orphaned infant, then his readiness to use non humans is simple discrimination, since adult apes, cats, mice, and other mammals are more aware of what is happening to them, more self-directing and, so far as we can tell, at least as sensitive to pain as any human infant…The experimenter, then, shows a bias in favour of his own species whenever he carried out an experiment on a non human for a purpose that he would not think justified him in using a human being at an equal or lower level of sentience, awareness, ability to be self-directing, etc…Experimenting on animals, and eating their flesh, are perhaps the two major forms of speciesism in our society.'[46]

Some philosophers however would argue that suffering experienced by animals is justifiable. For instance, some animal suffering is due to evolution and natural selection and nothing to do with human intervention. Indeed, what would the animal kingdom be like if evolution had not intervened to ensure the survival of certain species of animals and the death of others? Furthermore, because animals are undoubtedly different from us, many would argue that they cannot feel pain in the same way. Others would argue that animal suffering is caused by the perversion of the natural order that occurred after the Fall. Indeed, the fact that humans have the ability to make animals suffer is a necessary condition of our ability to have free will, just as is the ability to cause harm to fellow human beings.

Perhaps animal suffering only seems negative from our very limited perspective and in fact, there is an underlying purpose to it of which we are not aware.

Glossary

Holocaust	A term referring to the murder of millions of Jews, mostly in concentration camps, by the Nazi party during World War 2.
Theodicy	An attempt to justify the existence of God alongside the presence of evil.

The Augustinian and Irenaean Theodicies - Successes or Failures?

Aim

By the end of this chapter, you should have a good knowledge and understanding of how Augustine and Irenaeus attempted to justify God's existence alongside evil. You should also be able to attempt the examination questions which ask you to evaluate whether Augustine and Irenaeus were successful in their respective attempts. Therefore, you should have a good grasp of the various criticisms that have been made of each theodicy.

Two of the most important theodicies were developed by Augustine and Irenaeus. Despite being centuries old, they are still the most frequently quoted ways in which God's existence can be defended in the presence of evil. We shall spend the rest of the chapter outlining each theodicy in turn and evaluating their strengths and weaknesses. Let us turn first to the theodicy written by Augustine in the fourth century.

The Augustinian Theodicy (Saint Augustine: 354 – 430 CE)

Augustine believed in God and did not think that the Problem of Evil posed any threat to His existence. In fact, Augustine did not believe that there was any such thing as evil!

The Fall: Genesis 1–3

Many of Augustine's ideas were based on a very important text that can be found in the first three chapters of Genesis, the first book of the Bible. These chapters describe the creation of the world and of mankind. It is said that God created a world that was perfect; a world that even God Himself called 'good'. In this world, there was a beautiful garden called Eden which man (Adam) and woman (Eve) were given to live in. God warned Adam and Eve that, although they could live in the garden, if they ever ate an apple from the tree of the knowledge of good and evil, they would die.

Eve, however, was tempted by a serpent to eat from the tree and she gave Adam an apple to

Saint Augustine

eat also. In due course, God learned of their sin and cursed them in various ways. For Eve, God said that her pain would be multiplied in childbearing; and for Adam, that he would have difficulty in farming crops from the land. Furthermore, humanity would become mortal:

> 'You are dust and to dust you shall return.'
> (Genesis 3: 19)

Augustine believed that this original sin would be inherited by members of all future generations and therefore that everyone would be born with it. From this Fall of humanity, nothing would ever be the same; we would all be tainted by Adam and Eve's actions. It was here that evil was born.

Task

Reading Task	Read Genesis chapters 1 – 3.

An understanding of this story is very important for Augustine's theodicy. For Augustine, God created the world perfectly – it was good. As a consequence, Augustine denied the existence of evil. For Augustine, evil was *privatio boni*, the *privation of good*.

Evil as the Privation of Good

In order to understand what Augustine meant when he described evil as *privatio boni*, we must be able to distinguish between what is meant by there being an absence of something and there being a privation of something.

- **Absence**

    What features make up a human being? Well, most people would assume that the majority of us have a head, two arms and two legs. However, we would not expect a human to have fins! A human does not have to have fins to be human and so we say that a human has an absence of fins. In the same way, a fox has an absence of a trunk but obviously, a fox would not expect to have a trunk in the first place!

- **Privation**

    However, to have a privation of something is to lack something that is essential to the essence of that thing. So, if a human does not have an arm, then we would say that this human has a privation of an arm. Or, sickness is a privation of health. John Hick provides a good analogy to explain this term. He states that a glass can be half empty or half full and in this way, emptiness is not a thing in itself, but is merely a privation of drink. Similarly, blindness is a privation of sight.

    For Augustine, evil was a privation of good (privatio boni). Evil was not something that existed in itself, just as emptiness is not a thing that really exists. Rather, evil is a lack of goodness. Augustine states then, that evil is 'no substance, but the perversion of the will, turned aside from God … There can be no evil where there is no good ... Nothing evil exists in itself, but only as an evil aspect of some actual entity.[47]

For Augustine therefore, the world was created perfectly good and God had nothing at all to do with the introduction of evil. This was brought about by the actions of Adam and Eve when they disobeyed God. They were able to disobey God because they had the free will to do so.

Natural Evil

For Augustine, God also had nothing to do with the existence of natural evil. Augustine believed that natural evils were caused by the actions of fallen angels such as Lucifer (the Devil) who deliberately perpetrated such acts as a form of revenge on God.

Terence Tilley summarises Augustine's ideas in *The Evils of Theodicy*:

'Hence, all evil in the world is a result of sin. Natural evils, including much human suffering, result from angelic sin, and moral and spiritual evils from human sin. Those who are damned deserve eternal punishment because they have sinned. Their punishment restores order to the universe.'[48]

Criticisms of the Augustinian Theodicy

There have been many criticisms made of Augustine's ideas concerning the compatibility between God and evil. We shall look at the most important ones:

1. Many would question the idea of a Devil existing. Since God created the world, we would surely think that the Devil was under God's control also. As this must be the case, then this makes God partly responsible, at least, for the natural evils that take place in the world.

2. As we have seen, Augustine's ideas rest largely on the belief in the story written down in chapters 1-3 of the book of Genesis which describes the existence of a paradise state after the creation of the world. However, many philosophers such as John Hick would question this story from an evolutionary point of view. For example, we know that the evolution of man took place many millions of years after the creation of the earth.

3. Surely God could have created a world in which such evils would not happen. Indeed, if God created a good world, then surely the people he created would not be able to commit acts of evil.

4. F D E Schleiermacher (1768-1834) argued that God was responsible for evil. He argued that if God had created a perfect world, then it is illogical for it to then go wrong. Therefore, evil is the fault of God who caused it or enabled it to happen.

5. Also essential to the Augustinian theodicy is the belief in a Hell as a punishment for sin. However, the existence of Hell does seem to contradict the existence of a benevolent God and the creation of a perfect world.

Many would argue therefore that the Augustinian theodicy simply does not work; that his ideas are unscientific and, in many ways, naïve. Let us now look at the theodicy presented by Irenaeus and see if that is any more successful.

The Irenaean Theodicy (Irenaeus, Bishop of Lyons: 130 - 202 CE)

The Irenaean Theodicy is another very influential theodicy and carries much support today from philosophers such as Professor John Hick.

Read the following quotation taken from Genesis 1: 26:

Irenaeus, Bishop of Lyons.

> 'Then God said, "Let us make man in our image, after our likeness".'

Irenaeus believed that humans were created at an epistemic distance from God. He thought that although we were created in the image of God, we had to grow to become in his likeness, and so become one with God. For humanity to achieve this aim, we must live in a world which would enable us to grow and mature into spiritual beings. The kind of world which would enable mankind to do this would be a world full of temptation and danger i.e. the world we have now. Thus, the reason why evil exists is to enable us to grow as human beings so that we can become increasingly aware of, and like, God. Just like our parents sometimes allowed us to make our own mistakes, believing that it was in our own interests to learn for ourselves, so God creates a world for us in which we learn to grow and mature for ourselves.

John Hick agrees with Irenaeus but takes the theodicy one stage further. Hick argues that suffering provides a perfect opportunity for moral development or soul making. He states that a world like our own is preferable to any other:

> 'In eliminating the problems and hardships of an objective environment with its own laws, life would become like a dream in which delightfully but aimlessly we would float and drift at ease.'[49]

Furthermore, Hick believes that a future in Heaven will 'justify all that has happened on the way.'[50] We can enjoy a relationship with God because we have chosen this relationship. If we were not given the freedom to choose, we would simply be robots with God pulling the strings. Many would prefer to be free than to live the life of a robot!

Criticisms of the Irenaean Theodicy

Let us concentrate on the main criticisms that have been made of Irenaeus' Theodicy:

1. Surely, Irenaeus' Theodicy does not justify the killing of innocent children. Why should children be sacrificed to enable others to grow spiritually? Indeed, Ivan poses the problem of the six year old boy in *The Brothers Karamazov*. We could indeed ask how such an excruciating death could possibly enable him to grow and mature spiritually. Can we justify his death simply as a lesson to those around him?

2. If God is the omnibenevolent God modern religions believe him to be, then surely he could have made such moral spiritual virtues inbuilt in his creation.

3. Many would argue that if God was in any way caring, that he would enable his creation to learn such lessons in a far easier way. Many would state that some atrocities are too terrible to be justified in any way, even if we can all enjoy a great future in Heaven.

4. If we are meant to mature as a result of the temptations and troubles that surround us, then why do some people seem to have a much easier time than others?! Surely it would be fairer if we were all faced with the same experiences?

5. Furthermore, if we are all going to end up in Heaven anyway, what is the point in being good? Surely, this leaves us with no incentive to act in a morally good way.

6. Indeed, D Z Phillips argued that it is never justifiable to hurt anyone in order to help them. Therefore, according to Phillips, Irenaeus' theodicy fails to defend God in the presence of evil.

Seminar topic

Do you think that either Augustine or Irenaeus succeed in justifying God's existence alongside that of evil?

Tasks

Writing tasks	Outline how the existence of evil challenges belief in the very existence of God.
	Explain how the Augustinian theodicy tries to account for the co-existence of God and evil.
	Explain how the existence of suffering in the world challenges belief in God and outline the Augustinian response to that challenge. Discuss how successful the Augustinian response is in answering that challenge.
	Outline the evidence to support the claim that evil exists and explain the Irenaean theodicy which seeks to explain the existence of evil. Consider how far the Irenaean theodicy is a satisfactory explanation.

Glossary

Original Sin	The sin committed by Adam and Eve which is believed to have tainted every human being living subsequently.
The Fall	The sin committed by Adam and Eve which caused their downfall and expulsion from the Garden of Eden.

The Strengths and Weaknesses of Other Important Theodicies

Aim

This chapter will introduce you to other important theodicies that have been proposed in an attempt to justify God's existence alongside that of evil and suffering. By the end of this chapter, you should have a good knowledge and understanding of such theodicies as the Free Will Defence and Process Theodicy, as well as an ability to evaluate these theories.

Although the theodicies proposed by Augustine and Irenaeus have support even today, there have been theories proposed more recently which attempt to justify the existence of God alongside that of evil. We shall look at these major theodicies and as you work through them, try to think of the comments you would make about each theory. Do you think that each theory is successful in justifying the existence of evil? Or do you think that the suffering experienced by humanity can never be justified if God is meant to be all good?

Suffering as a form of punishment

The idea that suffering is a form of punishment, is very common in Biblical tradition. In the Bible, it is common to see God punishing those who have not been obedient to his will. Indeed, the two political catastrophes experienced by the Hebrews in the form of two exiles from their homeland were interpreted as punishment for the nation's sins.

The idea of suffering as a form of punishment is also linked to the thoughts of a theologian we have already considered: Augustine. According to Augustine, the sin committed by Adam has tainted us all and we are all therefore being punished because of this original sin. In a sense, we were all present with Adam when he disobeyed God, and for that reason, we must bear the consequences of his action. Thus, any suffering we experience is punishment for this original sin committed by Adam.

However, it is difficult to believe in this theory when we see the suffering experienced by innocent children. Many would argue that innocent children should not have to suffer as a consequence of a sin committed by Adam!

Nevertheless, Hindus would agree that suffering should be seen as a form of punishment. Hindus and Buddhists believe that suffering is a natural part of life that must be accepted; we are born in suffering and we die in suffering.

Read the following Buddhist story:

'Kisa Gotami had a beloved son, who, when he was just one year old, suddenly fell ill and died. Overcome with grief and unable to accept her son's death, she took the dead child in her arms and ran from house to house looking for medicine to restore the baby's life. No one knew what to do to console her, until someone mentioned that perhaps the Buddha might be able to help.

Kisa carried her son to the Buddha and begged for his help. He told her to go to the house of a family who had not experienced a death, and collect four or five mustard seeds. Convinced that this would bring her son back to life, she began her search.

Again and again doors were shut in her face. There was not one household which had not experienced the loss of a loved one. At last she understood what the Buddha was helping her to come to terms with – that death comes to all. She took her son away, and some time later returned to the Buddha to become one of his followers.'[51]

The Hindu and Buddhist response to suffering is different from Christian and Jewish ideas, insofar as they believe that suffering experienced by humans can be a result of sins committed in previous lives. Both Hindus and Buddhists believe in the law of Karma, i.e. everything we do has a consequence, either in this life or in future lives. Thus, those who experience suffering must have deserved this experience in some way. Suffering is a result of our actions, therefore; and as a consequence has nothing to do with the intervention or non-intervention of God. It is humans who must accept the responsibility for suffering on this planet. The only thing people who experience suffering can do, is to accept their suffering as part of their life and try to act in a selfless and loving way to others. By doing this, a Hindu or a Buddhist aims to improve his/her Karma in preparation for their next life.

Hindus and Buddhists believe that, ultimately, the only way to avoid suffering is to escape from the cycle of Samsara – the cycle of life, death and rebirth. If a Buddhist manages to do this, s/he will attain Nirvana and then Paranirvana, an assurance that no future lives will take place in the cycle of Samsara. For a Hindu, Moksha will be achieved – eternal unity with Brahman. Krishna says in the Bhagavad Gita 8: 15:

'Great souls who have become One with Me have reached the highest goal. They do not undergo re-birth, a condition which is impermanent and full of pain and suffering.'

Suffering as illusion

There are some people who argue that suffering is simply an illusion, a creation of the mind. For example, Mary Baker Eddy (1821-1910) was the founder of the Christian Science movement. According to Eddy, God was completely good and therefore goodness was real. As a consequence, evil and suffering were not real and were a result of ignorance of the true God. Thus, disease is just incorrect thinking and death is also an illusion, for belief in God gives one access to immortal life with God. Eddy believed that disease and sickness could be cured by mind healing, i.e. overcome by helping the sick person to understand that what s/he was feeling was not real and was a result of false belief.

Mary Baker Eddy

Eddy herself had experienced a life-changing event which she describes in *Miscellaneous Writings*. She claimed that she had fallen on an icy pavement in Massachusetts and received what doctors pronounced as a fatal injury. Eddy claimed:

'On the third day thereafter, I called for my Bible, and opened it at Matthew 9: 2. As I read, the healing Truth dawned upon my sense; and the result was that I rose, dressed myself, and ever after was in better health that I had before enjoyed.'[52]

For Christian Scientists, Jesus was the perfect model of somebody who transcended the illusion of sin and suffering because of his obedience to God. One can achieve the same by following his example.

The fact that Eddy herself died caused embarrassment to the Christian Science movement, for it could have implied she did not believe sufficiently to avoid bodily death. Indeed, many people would oppose the beliefs held by those following the Christian Science movement, believing instead that suffering is far from being an illusion and is something that causes untold pain for individuals and their families.

Seminar topic

Do you agree with Mary Baker Eddy that suffering is an illusion?

Suffering depends upon interpretation

Leading on from this theodicy, many would argue that to call something 'suffering' really depends upon your original perspective. For instance, many would argue that in terms of natural suffering volcanoes and earthquakes are, in themselves, neutral: there is nothing inherently evil in them – they only become evil when someone is hurt after coming into contact with them.

Herbert McCabe illustrates this idea effectively when he argues that if a lion eats a lamb, then this is obviously an example of suffering from the lamb's point of view. Nevertheless, from the perspective of the lion, filling his stomach with a lamb can only ever be a fulfilling experience!

Similarly, many would argue that the experience of suffering does not need to be negative. For instance, a belief in God may help a person who is suffering. Indeed, the thought that a life after death awaits can alleviate the distress of someone who is about to die, as well as that of their family and friends. For many, the belief in a life after death is the only way the deaths of innocent people can be tolerated. If one believes that this life on earth is all one can hope for, then the death of an innocent child could be unbearable. The belief that there is something awaiting the child after death can make this tragedy easier to cope with.

The free will defence

For Richard Swinburne, moral evil is largely the result of our own actions. Just like a parent, God gives us the ability to make our own mistakes. If God were to interfere with our actions all of the time, then we would be puppets without our own ability to lead our own lives. Therefore, although unfortunate, we must accept that we experience evil and suffering so that we can be free. Swinburne believes that our lives as free individuals are far more valuable than if they were controlled by God; in this way, we can approach God out of willingness rather than being forced to do so. As Swinburne himself says:

> 'The less he allows men to bring about large scale horrors, the less the freedom and responsibility he gives to them…[We are} asking that a God should make a toy-world, a world where things matter, but not very much; where we can choose and our choices can make a small difference but the real choices remain God's. For he simply would not allow us the choice of doing real harm, or through our negligence, allow real harm to occur. He would be like an overprotective parent who will not let this child out of his sight for a moment.'[53]

On the one hand, we can appreciate Swinburne's point. Surely it is better to be able to make our own decisions in life. Indeed, many would suggest that there is nothing worse than being told what to do and having your actions dictated by someone else. As a consequence, there are bound to be people hurt by the actions of those whose free will means that they have chosen to perform an action that someone else would not.

However, other philosophers would disagree! For example, Anthony Flew and J L Mackie argue that as God is believed to be an omnipotent being, then he would be able to create a world in which we have the freedom to do as we choose, but would always choose what is good! Indeed, Mackie argues that 'his failure to avail himself of this possibility is inconsistent with his being both omnipotent and wholly good.'[54] Everyone's nature would be to do what is good; and therefore, we would still have choice, but our choice would always result in the performance of good deeds.

Nevertheless, do we think that Flew and Mackie's criticism of Swinburne's ideas is adequate? Is our ability to do good on all occasions reflective of truly having free will? Many would argue that it is not. Furthermore, if God has really given us free will, then God cannot control our actions. If God did give us free will and was able to control our actions, then many would argue that this is not free will at all!

However, what about natural evil? Does Swinburne's justification of moral evil also justify the existence of natural evil? Surely our human actions do not cause the suffering caused by earthquakes and other natural disasters. Alvin Plantinga puts the existence of natural disasters down to the free will of other beings; particularly that of the Devil. The Devil is believed to be the chief of the fallen angels and it is the free will of these fallen angels that causes such devastation within the natural world.

Whether you agree with Plantinga's suggestion largely depends upon whether you believe in the existence of the Devil. Anthony Flew argues that no one has been able to prove that the Devil exists. Furthermore, we learn very little about the Devil and other angels within the Bible; they are only mentioned a few times within the whole text. It is difficult to see how an entire theodicy can be based upon hypothetical beings!

Seminar topic

Do you think that there is any proof that the Devil exists?

Process Theodicy

The Process Theodicy was first developed by A N Whitehead and later by D R Griffin in the twentieth century.

These philosophers argue that God has two distinct poles to his existence. One of these poles of God is within the universe. In other words, part of God is within the world and suffers alongside humanity. In this way, God is a co-sufferer. According to this theodicy, God did not create a perfect world, but he rather creates over time and brings order out of chaos. God did not create out of nothing, but worked with matter that was already in existence. Because of this, matter clearly had the capacity to turn away from God. This means that there is evil and suffering within the world and God is not powerful enough to stop it. Indeed, Whitehead believed that God was a fellow sufferer alongside humanity.

The theodicy argues that the universe is evolving and God is responsible for persuading the universe to become more harmonious. Nevertheless, God cannot make people reject their evil tendencies. Any evil that does occur is justified by the resulting harmony and order. Furthermore, it is better to live in a world in which evil occurs than not to live at all!

Many philosophers would argue, however, that the fact that the universe is evolving does not justify the suffering experienced by many innocent people. Furthermore, this theodicy does not justify the existence of natural evils. The theodicy also does not fit in with our Biblical understanding of God or creation. Many would argue that if we were to accept this theodicy, then we would have to completely rework our understanding of classical religious thought. Indeed, it is difficult to comprehend a God who did not create the world and who subsequently cannot control the world. This idea seems to contradict all that we understand about God's nature.

Task

Research task	Find out what else you can about Process Theodicy. Concentrate on the views of Whitehead and Griffin. Present your findings to the rest of the group.

Suffering as a test of faith

For many, the problems of suffering and evil remain as such. God's ways are ultimately mysterious and we should not attempt to understand why certain things happen. In the Old Testament, there is the story of Job (pronounced 'Jobe') who was afflicted with diseases after many of his family had been killed and his livelihood devastated. When Job finally calls upon God to explain why he had been afflicted in such a manner, God reveals creation to him and leaves Job with the unassailable conclusion that there is no way of understanding God's creation. Suffering and evil must be accepted and not questioned. Nevertheless, at the end of the story, God does reward Job for his faithfulness. Perhaps this leaves us with the impression that if those who suffer retain their faith, they will ultimately be rewarded for this, whether it be in this life or the next.

Similarly, for Muslims, suffering is a test sent by Satan. The way in which a person responds to this test will partly determine the rewards they will receive after death. Indeed, those who suffer and, as a result, turn away from Allah, can only expect punishment, but those who do not reject Allah can anticipate eternal reward:

'Be sure We shall test you with something of fear and hunger, some loss in goods or lives or the fruits of your toil, but give glad tidings to those who patiently persevere – who say when afflicted with calamity, "To God we belong and to Him is our return".'
Qur'an 2 :155-156[55]

The best of all possible worlds

Which universe shall I choose?

Leibniz (1646-1716) argued that when God created the world, He had the ability to choose from an infinite number of possible worlds to create. The fact that God chose to create this type of world does suggest that this world was the best choice. So, despite impressions, this world is the best possible world. Indeed, Swinburne, for example, argued that a world where there was death was a better world than a world where there was no death. For instance, if there was no death, then the world would be dominated by the old and furthermore, the knowledge that we are going to die makes us recognise that we must make the most of the time that we do have. Furthermore, death sets limits on how we treat each other. If there was no death and thus, no limit on the damage that we could do to our fellow man, then we would not know where to stop with the amount of harm that we inflict.

However, the idea that this is the best of all possible worlds is quite difficult to comprehend. Indeed, Voltaire parodied this idea in his book *Candide*: the two main characters, Candide and Mademoiselle Cunegonde, experience huge traumas and are reassured by Candide's tutor, Dr Pangloss, that at least they can be reassured that this is, after all, the best of all possible worlds.

Seminar topic

Do you think that any of these theodicies succeed in absolving God of any blame when it comes to the existence of evil and suffering?

Conclusion

Your discussion might well have highlighted the problems faced when attempting to justify the existence of God alongside evil. For many, the response to evil must be a practical one; we must concentrate our efforts on helping our fellow beings to cope with the adversity they experience on a daily basis. As B R Tilghman concludes:

'If there is a conclusion to be reached about the problem of evil, it is that the theoretical problem with which we began about whether or not four propositions are logically consisted is only the palest reflection of the struggles of life.'[56]

Tasks

Writing tasks	Explain what philosophers mean by 'the problem of evil' and outline the solution offered by Process Theodicy to this problem.
	Evaluate how successful Process Theodicy is in dealing with 'the problem of evil'.
	Explain the difficulties of attempts to reconcile animal suffering with the existence of God.
	Evaluate the claim that the Free Will Defence is a wholly unconvincing explanation.

Glossary

Illusion	Not real.
Karma	Literally meaning action, this word is used by Hindus and Buddhists to reflect the universal principle of cause and effect; every action has an effect in this life or in the next.
Moksha	A Hindu term describing the point at which the soul merges with Brahman.
Nirvana	Literally meaning blown out, describes the state of mind achieved by Buddhists who understand Buddhist truths. Paranirvana is the term to describe a person who, after attaining Nirvana during their lifetime, then dies a physical death.

Material for the Synoptic Module (A2)

The assessment for the Synoptic Module requires you to write an essay under controlled conditions on a specified aspect of either religious authority or religious experience or life, death and life after death. This essay should draw on material from at least two areas of study, because you are required to be able to sustain a critical line of argument which may involve comparing and contrasting different areas of study.

Religious Authority

For many religious believers, the use of rational argument to prove the existence of God is irrelevant. For such believers, arguments can only support their beliefs and give their ideas intellectual justification. For example, when Anselm, Archbishop of Canterbury, devised what we call now, the 'Ontological Argument' in the eleventh century, Anselm himself said that his intentions were not to convert people to Christianity but rather to give his own beliefs intellectual justification.

For the majority of believers, it is the experience they have of God and the subsequent relationship they have with God which is of most importance.

Religious Experience

As hinted at above, many religions based their belief in God upon experiences they have of God. Many believers purport to have had visions of God or experienced miracles which have proved to them that God exists. In the New Testament, for example, we hear of Saul of Tarsus who experiences a vision and hears God speaking to him. This experience converts him to Christianity and from this point on, we know of Saul by the name of Paul, who then goes on to write many of the letters in the New Testament.

However, many philosophers would doubt the validity of such experiences. Many experiences lack objective verification and the lack of eyewitness accounts succeed, in the views of many, to disprove the validity of such experiences. Some psychologists would even argue that the experience of Saul was due to a mental breakdown caused by a crisis in his life. This could well have been brought about by his persecution of the Christians.

Ideas of Life, Death and Life After Death

Believers within every religion live with the hope that they will experience some kind of life that will continue after death. For most religions, the kind of life this will be depends upon the individual's actions during life. Some religions believe that what one does during life dictates the kind of life one is born into in the ongoing wheel of Samsara. For others, life's good deeds are rewarded with an eternal life in the presence of God.

However, many philosophers would question the validity of such beliefs. Philosophers such as Descartes have discussed the relationship between mind and body and therefore what might conceivably live on after physical death. Is there such a thing as the soul or is it interchangeable with our understanding of the mind? Can the soul continue after death without any attachment to a physical body? All of these questions will be discussed in relation to this topic.

References

[1] *The Bible, Revised Standard Version*, HarperCollins Publishers, 1971.

[2] Karl Marx and Friedrich Engels, *On Religion,* New York, Schocken Books, 1964, p.42.

[3] Atkins, Peter, and Ward, Keith, *Religion and Science*, in *Dialogue*, Issue 10, April 1998.

[4] Paley, William, *Natural Theology*, London, 1802.

[5] ibid.

[6] ibid.

[7] ibid.

[8] Quoted from *A Short Scheme of the True Religion*, in Brewster, D. *Memoirs of the Life, Writings and Discoveries of Sir Isaac Newton*, Edinburgh, T. Constable, 1850, Vol. 1. pp 347-348.

[9] Aquinas, Thomas, *Summa Theologica*, Eyre & Spottiswoode, 1972.

[10] Hume, David, *Dialogues Concerning Natural Religion* (1779), edited with an introduction by Normal Kemp Smith, London, Thomas Nelson, 1935.

[11] Taken from a lecture given at Chestnut Hill College in Philadelphia on November 28th, 2001, entitled *Theology and Science in the 21st Century*. (www.pc4rs.org/newsletters/2001_03/Polkinghorne.html) 10th April 2003.

[12] Swinburne, Richard, *The Existence of God*, Oxford University Press, 1979.

[13] ibid.

[14] Crowder, Colin, *The Design Argument*, in *Dialogue,* Issue 1, November 1993.

[15] Kant, Immanuel, *Critique of Pure Reason* (translated by Norman Kemp Smith), St. Martin's Press, 1965.

[16] Crowder, Colin, *The Design Argument Part 2 : Why It Fails*, in *Dialogue,* Issue 2, April 1994.

[17] Hume, David, *Dialogues Concerning Natural Religion*, (1779) edited with an introduction by Normal Kemp Smith, London, Thomas Nelson, 1935.

[18] ibid.

[19] Crowder, Colin, *The Design Argument Part 2 : Why It Fails*, in *Dialogue,* Issue 2, April 1994.

[20] Hume, David, *Dialogues Concerning Natural Religion*, (1779) edited with an introduction by Normal Kemp Smith, London, Thomas Nelson, 1935.

[21] Mill, John Stuart, *Three Essays on Religion*, London, Longmans, Green, Reader, and Dyer, 1874.

[22] Dawkins, Richard, *The Blind Watchmaker*, London, Penguin Books, 1988.

[23] Palmer, Michael, *The Question of God*, Routledge, 2001.

[24] Aquinas, Thomas, *Summa Theologica*, Eyre & Spottiswoode, 1972.

[25] ibid

[26] ibid

[27] Leibniz, Gottfried, *Theodicy*, 1710.

[28] Craig, William Lane, *Kalam Cosmological Argument*, London, Macmillan, 1979.

[29] Broadcast in 1948 on the Third Programme of the BBC. Published in *Humanitas* (Manchester) and reprinted in Russell, Bertrand, *Why I Am Not a Christian*, London, George Allen & Unwin, 1957.

[30] Kant, Immanuel, *Critique of Pure Reason* (translated by Norman Kemp Smith), St. Martin's Press, 1965.

[31] Hawking, Stephen, *A Brief History of Time*, Bantam Press, 1988.

[32] Mill, John Stuart, *Three Essays on Religion*, London, Longmans, Green, Reader, and Dyer, 1874.

[33] Broadcast in 1948 on the Third Programme of the BBC. Published in *Humanitas* (Manchester) and reprinted in Russell, Bertrand, *Why I Am Not a Christian*, London, George Allen & Unwin, 1957.

[34] Flew, Anthony, *God and Philosophy*, London, Hutchinson, 1966.

[35] Hume, David, *Dialogues Concerning Natural Religion*, (1779) edited with an introduction by Normal Kemp Smith, London, Thomas Nelson, 1935.

[36] Kant, Immanuel, *Critique of Pure Reason* (translated by Norman Kemp Smith), St. Martin's Press, 1965.

[37] Broadcast in 1948 on the Third Programme of the BBC. Published in *Humanitas* (Manchester) and reprinted in Russell, Bertrand, *Why I Am Not a Christian*, London, George Allen & Unwin, 1957.

[38] ibid.

[39] ibid.

[40] Webber, Jonathan, *Cosmological Arguments for the Existence of God*, in *Dialogue*, Issue 5, November 1995.

[41] Palmer, Michael, *The Question of God*, Routledge, 2001.

[42] Based on data from the 2001 Summary Report on research carried out by the Department of Health; and the National HIV and Syphilis Sero-Prevalence Survey of Women Attending Public Antenatal Clinics in South Africa.

[43] Wiesel, Elie, *Night*, New York, Hill and Wang, Avon Books, 1958.

[44] Lactantius, *De Ira Dei*, 13.

[45] Dostoevsky, Fyodor M., *The Brothers Karamazov*, translated by Richard Pevear and Larissa Volokhonsky, New York, Knopf, 1992.

[46] Regan, Tom, Singer, Peter, (eds), *Animal Rights and Human Obligations* (Second Edition), Prentice Hall, 1989.

[47] St. Augustine, *The Confessions of Saint Augustine*, (397) translated by Edward Pusey, New York, P.F. Collier & Son, 1909-1914.

[48] Tilley, Terence, *The Evils of Theodicy*, Washington, Georgetown University Press, 1991.

[49] Hick, John, *Evil and the God of Love*, Macmillan, 1978.

[50] ibid.

[51] taken from Cole, Owen, W., *Moral Issues in Six Religions*, Heinemann Educational, 1991 (page 20).

[52] Eddy, Mary Baker, *Miscellaneous Writings*, Boston, First Church, 1977.

[53] Swinburne, Richard, *The Existence of God*, Oxford, Clarendon Press, 1979.

[54] Mackie, J. L, *Evil and Omnipotence*, Mind, 1955.

[55] *The Koran*, Oxford University Press, 1964.

[56] Tilghman, B.R., *An Introduction to the Philosophy of Religion*, Blackwell Publishers Ltd, 1994.

Bibliography

Clarke, P. J., *Questions About God : A Guide for A/AS Students*, Stanley Thornes, 1999

Cole, P., *Philosophy of Religion*, Hodder & Stoughton, 1999

Davies, B., *An Introduction to the Philosophy of Religion*, OUP, 1993

Esler, P. F. (ed), *Christianity for the Twenty-first Century*, T & T Clark, 1998

Hick, J., *The Existence of God*, Macmillan, 1964

Le Poidevin, R., *Arguing For Atheism*, Routledge, 1996

Mackie, J., *The Miracle of Theism*, Oxford, 1982

Mitchell, B. (ed), *The Philosophy of Religion*, OUP, 1981

Pailin, D., *Groundwork of Philosophy of Religion*, Epworth, 1986

Palmer, M., *The Question of God*, Routledge, 2001

Pinchin, C., *Issues in Philosophy*, Macmillan, 1990

Tilghman, B. R., *An Introduction to the Philosophy of Religion*, Blackwell, 1994

Vardy, P., *The Puzzle of Evil*, HarperCollins, 1992

Vardy, P., *The Puzzle of God*, HarperCollins, 1999